Street Cop

Street Cop

Davɪᴅ Spᴇʟʟ

RESOURCE *Publications* · Eugene, Oregon

STREET COP

Resource Publications
An Imprint of Wipf and Stock Publishers
199 W. 8th Ave., Suite 3
Eugene, OR 97401
www.wipfandstock.com

ISBN 13: 978-1-60899-696-4

Manufactured in the U.S.A.

To Sarah Shackleford
And
Rachel Hanna

I am blessed to have such incredible daughters!
I pray that your children will bring you as much joy as
you have brought me.

Contents

Preface

I HAVE BEEN IN Law Enforcement for almost thirty years. I have been blessed with a wonderful career that has been full of incredible memories. That is what these pages contain. As I look back over my Law Enforcement career, I don't know that I would have changed a thing. I am a street cop. My entire career has been one in which I have put on a uniform everyday, got into my marked police car, and gone to work, serving the citizens and residents of our community. I have spent the bulk of my time with the police department working at the various precincts as a uniformed officer, a Field Training Officer, a Shift Supervisor, and ultimately as a Watch Commander. I also did tours in two different Special Operations Units. Both of these were uniformed, enforcement positions. One sad reality is that the higher you go in rank, the less actual enforcement that you are involved in. As a Lieutenant, I don't get into nearly the amount of "stuff" that I did as an Officer, a Corporal, or a Sergeant.

What follows in these pages are some of the interesting calls and incidents that I was involved in over the course of my career. I have not tried to organize them chronologically. Instead, they are loosely grouped by the type of incident. They are all true. In many cases, I have supplemented my memory with the actual police reports and other documents. I have chosen to only use officer's first names because I do not want to embarrass anyone. I have changed suspect's names and made minor changes to some locations. I also cleaned up the language so as not to offend. Some of these stories will make you laugh and you may find some of them to be disturbing. At any rate, I hope you enjoy them. More importantly, though, I hope that through these pages you will develop an even greater appreciation for the men and women in blue who are out on the streets of America 24/7 protecting our communities from predators.

I would like to express my thanks, love, and respect for the incredible men and women that I have been privileged to work with over course of my career. Thanks for watching my back on bad calls, sharing a cup of coffee with me on those long winter's nights on third shift, and thanks especially for the part each of you played in writing this book.

David Spell
Buford, Georgia
2010

"Shoot Me!"

"SHOOT ME, SHOOT ME," the short, shirtless, muscular Korean man said as he walked slowly towards Officer Jay and me. He was holding a large kitchen knife and we could see the blood trickling down his chest and abdomen from where he had been cutting himself. Jay and I both drew our pistols and took a step backwards, preparing to defend ourselves.

We had gotten a 911 call in February of 1991, at around midnight, to this quiet Lilburn neighborhood from the Korean man's adult son. The man had two sons at the house, both in their mid twenties. They both spoke English, but their mother, who was also there, only spoke Korean. When Jay and I had arrived at the residence, the two sons met us outside. They told us that their father was depressed about losing his job and other personal issues. He had been drinking all evening, which only increased his depression. We also found out later that he was mixing alcohol and prescription pain pills which made a bad situation even worse. The sons had been sitting with their father, but he had still managed to slip into the kitchen and get a knife. That was when he had said he was going to kill himself.

The two sons had immediately sprung into action and wrestled the knife away from their father. They had called 911 because they wanted us to take him to get some help. Officer Jay and I went into the house and made contact with the man. He was about fifty years old but appeared fit and very intoxicated. Jay found out that the man had been in the Korean version of the Marines. Jay was a former United States Marine himself and this created an opportunity for the two to talk.

While Jay was talking to the father, I spoke to the two sons. They explained that they were worried that their dad really was going to kill himself if we did not help him. The problem is, thanks to the lawmakers in Georgia, it is not against the law to kill yourself and threatening or even attempting suicide does not provide grounds for involuntary committal. The family's options were fairly limited. If their dad would consent to go voluntarily to the hospital, we would take him. If he refused, there was not much that we could legally do. Another option was that if he committed some criminal offense we could arrest him and take him to the hospital for psychiatric evaluation. Up to this point, however, the subject had not broken any laws.

After Jay had talked to the father and I had spoken to the two sons, we compared notes. I told him that the sons wanted their dad taken into custody to get him some help but that I had told them that we could not do that at this point. Jay said that he had a good conversation with the man. Jay asked him if he would be willing to go to the hospital and get checked out. The father told Jay that he did not need any help and he was okay now. Talking with another military man had made him feel better. He assured Jay that he would not try and harm himself again. He even said that he might go see his doctor tomorrow if he wasn't feeling better.

Both Jay and I felt that we had calmed the situation down as much as we could. We told the sons to keep an eye on their dad and to call us back if they felt that they needed us. We both left the house feeling that we had handled the call and done our good deed for the night. We could not have been more wrong.

As we were backing out of the driveway, one of the suicidal Korean's sons came running down the driveway, yelling for us to stop. "He's got another knife and he is stabbing himself!" Jay and I rushed back into the house and found the Korean man sitting on a couch in the living room holding a large knife. He was cutting himself on his chest and abdomen but did not appear to be feeling any pain.

When he saw that the police were back in his house, he stood up and started walking slowly towards us, holding the knife out in front of him. "Shoot me, shoot me," he pleaded with us. Jay backed up as far as he could. The suicidal man's two sons and his wife were standing behind him, pressing around him. They saw us draw our guns and knew what was about to happen. They were screaming, pleading in Korean for the man to stop and put the knife down. Jay and I both yelled at the man to drop the knife. Instead, he kept walking slowly towards us, saying in heavily accented and slurred English, "Shoot me!"

Now I know that in the movies and on television, knives are not really considered a threat. The hero usually kicks the knife out of the bad guys hand or grabs the hand with knife and twists it until the knife falls out. These "Hollywood encounters" do a great disservice to those in Law Enforcement. If an officer has to shoot someone who attacks them with a knife, they are often second guessed by the press and citizen advocate groups, none of which have ever been in a deadly encounter with someone who wanted to kill them.

I have been involved in some type of martial arts for most of my life and am proficient with empty hand strikes, kicks, joint locks, pressure points and many types of weapons. In a real encounter, however, I am not about to fight someone armed with a knife. If you have ever seen anyone carved up by someone who is proficient with a knife, you will understand why Jay and I were about to shoot this drunk, suicidal Korean.

As the family members continued to scream in Korean over Jay's shoulder, I knew he was going to have a tougher time making a shot. He was being jostled as the two sons and the wife tried get around him. Jay was using his body, trying to shield the family from getting in the way. However, I knew that it was a matter of seconds before Jay was going to be forced to fire his Smith & Wesson 9mm pistol.

I had backed up against a wall and slid sideways down a few feet to get a better angle. I was now to the side of suicidal man. Because of Jay's position, I knew that it would be better if I took the shot. I raised my Smith & Wesson .45 caliber pistol and put the front sight on the man's right ear and started to squeeze the trigger. The man with the knife was less than fifteen feet away, much too close. He continued to shuffle towards us pleading, "Shoot me!"

As the hammer was coming back on my double action, semi-automatic pistol, I realized for the first time, that the Korean man did not know I existed. His attention was fixed completely on Jay. Maybe he felt that it was more honorable to be killed by a United States Marine than by his own hand. Unless he turned to his right, the suicidal man would walk right by me.

I observed all of this in a split second. I released the trigger of my pistol and holstered it. I drew my police baton or "nightstick." I knew I was going against the Police Tactics Manual, but I was willing to try one time to disarm the guy. Jay and I both knew we would have been completely justified in shooting this guy. In that split second, however, I thought maybe we could avoid killing him. Justified or not, shooting him would create a lot of emotional trauma for us, the Korean family, and would mean a lot of paperwork.

The man's right side was to me and the large knife was in his right hand. He had the knife raised and pointing at Jay. The family was still screaming in Korean and Jay was still yelling at him to drop the knife but I had blocked it out. I knew Jay was getting ready to shoot so I needed to act fast. I stepped forward and in one motion, raised my nightstick and brought it crashing down on the suicidal man's right forearm. I hit him just as hard as I could, knowing that if I missed or did not disarm him, I could slide out of the way and let Jay shoot him.

When the nightstick smashed into the man's forearm, the knife went flying across the living room. I wasn't about to give him a chance to retrieve it so I dropped the nightstick behind me and reached over and grabbed the guy behind the neck with my right hand. I then pulled forward on the man's neck and used my right leg to kick his legs in the opposite direction. The result was that the Korean was slammed down hard to the floor on his face. I dropped both knees into his back. Jay had responded immediately to my nightstick strike. As soon as the knife was out of the man's hand, he was holstering his pistol and stepping in. He followed my lead and dropped onto the man's back so that we could keep him pinned to the floor long enough to get him handcuffed.

Now Jay and I are both big boys. I am about six foot two and, at the time was about two hundred and twenty pounds out of uniform. With all of my equipment on, I tipped the scales at about two hundred and forty pounds. Jay is about six foot one and outweighs me by about twenty pounds. With us on this guy's back, he wasn't going anywhere. He struggled a bit as we tried to get him handcuffed but we got him secured. Then we both just sat there for a minute staring at each other and catching our breaths, knowing how close we had been to killing this man.

Jay now had a criminal charge (Aggravated Assault on Police Officers) and took the man to the hospital for psychiatric evaluation and involuntary committal. About a week later, Jay got a phone call from one of the suicidal man's sons. Jay asked him how his father was. He said, "Well, his right forearm is broken and he is in a cast. He is going to have to have back surgery in the next few weeks from where you guys jumped on his back. He has several vertebrae that are messed up." Jay did not like where this conversation was going. He thought that the next thing he was going to hear is that we were going to be sued.

Instead, the young Korean man continued, "But please don't worry about all of that. It is okay. I want to thank you for not killing my father. I know you could have but instead, chose to use other means to get him the help that he needed. These injuries will heal. I am sorry that you had to see my father in that condition. He is a good man." Jay thanked the young man for his call. Officer Jay received the Departmental Officer of the Month Award for this incident. I received a Letter of Commendation for my part.

This encounter drove home to me more clearly than ever before the necessity of good, consistent training. In a physical confrontation, most techniques do not work like we intend them to. I know that is hard to believe because Jack Bauer always lands his punch or kick on television, but in real life, it is just as common to miss or to have the technique not work. I was very fortunate in this situation that the two techniques that I used, the baton strike and the leg sweep, worked perfectly and allowed us to save a life rather than take one.

2

Police Academy

I ENTERED THE POLICE Academy in early 1984. My wife, Annie, and I had just spent a year in Ghana, West Africa doing missionary work. Living in Africa was a tremendous experience but the hot climate and lack of good, fattening American food had me looking like a six foot two, one hundred and sixty pound scarecrow. I also had long hair and a beard. When I reported for duty to the Police Academy, these were gone and I looked presentable. I had just turned twenty one years of age.

I was one of the twenty recruits in Gwinnett Police Academy Number 16. It would be almost four months before we would graduate and be "real" police officers. The Academy was run somewhat like a military boot camp. Our lead instructor, Officer Hal, had been a drill sergeant in the army and he liked to remind us of that. Every day included a lot of PT (Physical Training). We ran at least two miles every day and sometimes as many as four or five. We did pushups, sit ups, and all kinds of other calisthenics. We also had a sadistic obstacle course that we had to run regularly.

This PT had its desired effect. When the academy was over, I was a solid one hundred and eighty pounds. It would not be until a few years later that I started lifting weights seriously and putting on some more muscular size and strength. But for the time being, I would be ready for life on the street.

The core of the Police Academy was the classroom training. A few of the classes made a lasting impact on us. We had several weeks of Criminal Procedures, Criminal Law, and Traffic Law. These were three very important blocks of instruction and the person they had to teach it to us was a legend in the Georgia law enforcement community.

Tate Brown quickly became our favorite instructor. He was delightfully profane, unabashedly irreverent, and politically incorrect on a scale that would prevent him from even entering the Police Training Center today, much less teach there. He had been in law enforcement in several different agencies for close to thirty years. At the time he taught my class, he was working in some capacity for the governor.

The several weeks of training in the various laws, and how to enforce them, are typically some of the dullest and driest weeks of the Academy. It was not like that with Tate. From day one, he had us spell-bound with his stories. For every law that he discussed, he had a story to illustrate it. We laughed and laughed, but we also learned. We could not wait to get out on our own and start enforcing the Law. Years later, I took a week long refresher block on Criminal Procedures. It was taught by someone from the District Attorney's Office. I thought that week would never end. He was not that bad of an instructor but there will never be another Tate Brown.

Another one of the big blocks of instruction at the Academy was in Defensive Tactics. This lasted about two weeks. For this class, they again brought in an outside instructor. This time it was Special Agent Gary of the FBI. I asked Officer Hal why they had to bring someone from the FBI to teach us how to fight. I asked him, "Do we not have anyone in our department that knows how to fight?"

He answered in that sweet, condescending tone of his, "Just asking that question shows ignorant you are, Spellman (one of the many variations of my last name that he used). But since you are so stupid, I'll try and enlighten you. The reason that we have the FBI teach Defensive Tactics is so that when you go and out beat somebody up and use excessive force, we can say that we had the FBI show him the right way to do it but he is a loose cannon and wanted to do things his own way."

Having not learned that the better part of valor often means biting your tongue, I asked another question, "But couldn't the Department could still do that even if they had one of our own instructors teaching us?"

In his patient and understanding way, Officer Hal exploded, "Spellbound, this is the FBI! They are the premier law enforcement agency in the United States. You should consider it a privilege to be taught by them. You should consider it a privilege to even be in the same room with one of them."

I could not resist one more question. "Officer Hal, does the FBI get in a lot of fights?" I mean when you watch them on the news, they take like fifty agents to go and get one little accountant for embezzlement or something. I know that the war on terror has changed things for them, but that was my perception back in the 80s. Officer Hal did not even answer me this time. He just walked away shaking his head and muttering.

Special Agent Gary was definitely special. He was as close to insane as anyone I have ever met who carried a badge and a gun. I doubt he could have passed the psychological test that I had had to pass to get hired. He did not really teach us anything. He had us wrestle around and beat each other up on the mats. That was good fun but there was no real instruction. He would stand off to the side smoking. Occasionally, he would stop us and tell us some story from his past that did not relate to anything we were supposed to be doing.

People have asked me over the years if they teach you how to fight in the Police Academy. My standard answer has always been, "They teach you just enough to get hurt." In other words, if you don't know how to fight and defend yourself to begin with, the little bit you get in the Police Academy is not really going to help you. The defensive tactics training is much better today, with an emphasis on ground fighting, use of pressure points and learning how to strike properly. Defensive tactics have to be practiced regularly, however, or they will disappear.

Agent Gary also tried to show us how to handcuff properly. I say "tried" because in the real world, your opponent is seldom compliant or letting you win. We spent so many hours handcuffing each other that our wrist bones were bruised and sore. One of the highlights of the DT class was watching Recruit Paul (a guy) fight with Recruit Jody (a girl). The goal was to get the other recruit down on the floor and then hand-cuff them. Paul never was able to wrestle Jody to the floor or get her handcuffed. She, however, pretty much thrashed him every time they tangled. When it was Jody's turn to be the aggressor, she had no trouble at all body slamming Paul and then handcuffing him. It was pretty em-barrassing for Paul but we all enjoyed the show.

Recruit Paul stuck around for a few years but never really fit in. He moved to a smaller department and had a successful career there. I don't think he had to get into too many fights. Recruit Jody worked the street for a couple of years until she got pregnant. After that, she worked in a non-enforcement capacity for a while but then quit to be a full time mom.

Another area of DT Training that Agent Gary instructed us in was that of disarming techniques, as in taking away a gun or knife from someone. I said earlier that Agent Gary was insane. We had already suspected it from some of the things he had said and had us do. Now he confirmed it. As he taught us how to take a gun away from someone, he prefaced it by saying, "I know that these techniques work because I always practice them against a loaded gun and I'm still alive."

We must not have heard him right. One of the recruits asked for clarification, "Special Agent Gary, did you say that you practiced disarming techniques with a loaded gun?"

Agent Gary puffed out his chest and said, "Oh yeah! Anybody can practice with an unloaded gun. You know the gun is unloaded and the adrenaline really doesn't get flowing. But when my training partner points that loaded and cocked revolver at my head all my senses come alive. If I don't execute my disarming technique properly, I'm a dead man."

There was a stunned silence. We were just recruits but we knew that this violated every firearms safety rule that we had been taught. Was this the way they did at the FBI? Is that the way that they taught disarming in their academy? Was this one of things we were supposed to be learning from "the premier law enforcement agency in the United States?" And this crazy man was going to show us "the right way" to do things?

We practiced the various disarming techniques that Agent Gary showed us. Of course, we used non-firing, training guns and rubber knives. We continued to enjoy watching Paul and Jody working together. He was never able to disarm her but she took away his gun every time they practiced together. Agent Gary never encouraged us to practice with loaded guns. He just let us know that we were not getting the full effect by using training guns. I think our class was one of the last ones in which the FBI taught DT. Before long, we had our own DT Instructors teach us "the right way."

Firearms' training was one of my favorite parts of the Police Academy. At the time I went through, we were carrying Smith & Wesson .357 magnum revolvers. We shot a lot of ammo as we worked towards qualification day. If you didn't qualify, they could wash you out or make you go through Academy again. We had some borderline shooters that just managed to squeak by, but we got everyone through. I always enjoyed shooting and shot pretty well.

While the bulk of firearms training was with our revolvers, we also trained with the pump-action 12 gauge shotgun. The Department did not issue everyone a shotgun. If you wanted to carry one, you had to buy your own. Everyone, however, had to be trained on how to use the shotgun. I bought my own shotgun and started carrying it as soon as I could.

The guy who was over the Firearms Training Unit was Sergeant Mike. He was a very unpleasant person. He might be described as moody, but he really only had one mood and that was a bad one. He could really shoot, however, and competed in a lot of tournaments. He was actually a pretty good teacher as well when he wasn't brooding or pouting. At the same time, he was quick to criticize, belittle, and berate us recruits. If you got on his bad side, he was unmerciful.

On one of the days that we were learning shotgun, we went to an outdoor skeet range to shoot. It was a lot of fun. Skeet shooting is excellent training. Sergeant Mike had been bragging about how he could shoot skeet with his revolver. None of us believed that that was even possible and we told him so. Right after we got to the skeet range, Sergeant Mike gave it a go and missed six out of six with his revolver. We enjoyed seeing him fail after all the abuse that we had taken. He did not enjoy being laughed at by a bunch of recruits and stomped away. He pouted the rest of the day. He let the assistant instructors work with us as we shot skeet.

Before we left the shotgun range for the day, Sergeant Mike wanted to try one more time to shoot skeet with his revolver. We were all hoping he would strike out again. Instead, he hit five out of six clay birds with his revolver. That still ranks as one of the most impressive things I have ever seen anyone do with a handgun.

About half way though the Police Academy, we lost a guy. A citizen saw him drinking beer in the parking lot of a shopping center with some of his friends. That would not have been such a big deal except for the fact that he was still in his police uniform. There is just no cure for stupid. He was gone the next day.

I was never much of a partier so I skipped the ones that were thrown by Academy mates. I wasn't much of a drinker and had heard stories about the amount of alcohol some of these folks could consume. One Monday morning my decision to skip the weekend's festivities were justified. Recruit Ken came in with a busted up face. His eye was black and still swollen. I asked him, "What happened to you?"

He said, "Ah, Greg punched me for no reason."

There was a little more to the story than that. Ken had become very intoxicated at the party and made a few lewd remarks to Recruit Greg's wife. Greg did not appreciate that and punched Ken in the face. The fact that neither man was disciplined for the incident indicates that Ken probably got what he deserved.

A number of years later, Ken's drinking would cost him his job as a police officer. He was off-duty and driving home after a night on the town when he got stopped by one of our officers. Common sense will tell you that this not the time to be a smart ass. This is the time to be humble and contrite and hope the officer will help you out. In Ken's case, the alcohol had driven common sense out the window and smart ass won out. Ken was uncooperative and verbally abusive towards the officer that had stopped him. He got arrested for Driving Under the Influence and resigned in lieu of termination a couple of days later.

Finally, after four long months, it was time for us to graduate from the Police Academy and become full-fledged police officers. We had lost three other recruits over the course of the academy for one thing or another and we graduated sixteen. We had been issued all of our equipment and a marked police car. My first patrol car was a 1979 Chevrolet Impala. I was thrilled. I was excited. I was ready to go to work.

My Field Training Officer was Officer Steve. We rode together for two and a half weeks. Today, recruits usually ride with three or four FTOs for around twelve weeks. It was not as structured back then. Officer Steve taught me how to work vehicle accidents. He taught me how to make traffic stops. He taught me how to handle domestic calls. He also taught me the real important stuff, like which restaurants gave the police a discount.

In our first week together, Steve was still driving and I was observing. By the end, I would be driving and he would be observing. This first week, though, we got a call to a Theft in Progress. A male was observed stealing things from behind a house. The caller gave us a good description of the suspect. As we pulled up, the suspect came around the side of the house carrying his stolen goods. He saw us, dropped the property and started running. Without waiting to be told what to do, or asking permission from my FTO, I was out of the car and chasing the thief.

I chased him across the yard and through the woods. It was about 11:00 in the morning so I had no trouble keeping the suspect in sight. After about one hundred yards, he started slowing up. As I closed on him, he started yelling, "I give up!" I took him to the ground as we had been taught in the academy and applied the handcuffs. I quickly searched him and found a few other stolen items concealed in his clothes.

Only after I had the guy under control, did I realize that I was by myself. Where was Officer Steve? I got the suspect up and escorted him out of the woods. Steve had pulled the police car around to where we were. When he saw that I had caught the thief, his face lit up in a big grin. "Good job!" he said. We arrested the guy and took him to jail. This was good experience for a new guy like me.

When we went in at the end of our shift to turn our paperwork in, Officer Steve told everyone about me chasing this thief down and catching him. The Sergeant and the Lieutenant both congratulated me. Even several of the old crusty veteran officers nodded approvingly at me. What I didn't realize until later was that I had just passed my first real test. Sure, there were a number of things that we were tested on in the Police Academy. Now, however, it was for real. The tests that I would be taking every day had life and death consequences. Before the older guys would accept us young, wet behind the ears recruits, we had to prove ourselves. They had to know that they could trust us. By chasing down a criminal and catching him, I had shown them that I was going to be OK.

3

Knock Out

I‌T WAS ABOUT 12:30 at night in mid April, 1985. I was working the midnight shift and received a call to a drunk person causing a disturbance at a nearby Kroger, a twenty four hour grocery store. There were several people standing in front of the store as I pulled up. Officer Paul, my academy mate, (the same one who got beat up by the girl in DT) joined me at the scene.

One of the people identified himself as the night manager of the Kroger. He pointed at a man standing a few feet away on the sidewalk and said that he was intoxicated and causing a scene inside the store. He had made a few lewd remarks towards some of the female cashiers and customers. He had refused to leave when ordered to do so and had also threatened to "beat the hell out of" several of the male employees who were trying to get him to leave the store. The manager had then called the police.

At this point, during my conversation with the manager, the intoxicated man staggered over and started yelling at the Kroger employees. The man was about six foot one and weighed around one hundred and eighty pounds. He looked to be around fifty years of age but was athletic looking. I found out later he was a retired navy chief.

The drunk man pointed at the store manager and said, "He's bothering me."

I told the drunk man that he needed to calm down or he would be arrested. Instead of calming down, though, he pushed past me and advanced towards the store manager snarling, "You're a stupid punk and I'm going to teach you a lesson!" As the drunk man drew back his right arm to punch the store manager, I grabbed his left arm and pulled him off balance. I could see that he had a round object in his right hand but I did not know what it was.

My police car was just a few feet away. I pulled the drunk towards it intending to handcuff him and get him in the car before he had a chance to attack me. This was one of those situations where even though I had another officer there with me, I was still pretty much by myself. Officer Paul was a really nice guy but was not someone you wanted to have with you in a fight.

Just as we got to my police car, the drunk jerked away from me and drew back his right hand to punch me. I saw it coming and fired a straight left punch that caught the guy square on the jaw. It was like someone had flicked the light switch in his brain to the "Off" position. He was unconscious before he crashed to the pavement. When he fell, he landed heavily and the back of his head bounced when it hit the pavement. I immediately rolled him over and handcuffed him. I quickly checked him for weapons and then inspected the object that had fallen from his right hand. It was a rock, the size of a softball. It weighed about one pound. That was what this guy was going to hit the Kroger manager and me with if he had had the chance.

I checked the unconscious man and found that he was breathing okay but was still out and our efforts to revive him were not having much effect. Officer Paul called an ambulance and I got statements from all the witnesses. One of the witnesses told me that the man had been at the Derby Food & Spirits, a classy establishment a few doors down from the Kroger. He had been there for a couple of hours drinking and becoming more belligerent with every beer. He had tried to vandalize the jukebox and was barely prevented from turning it over by security.

When the drunk man started harassing some of the female customers in the bar, the bouncers told him it was time to leave. He really did not want to leave the bar, however, and security had to throw him out. Outside the bar, he had thrown several objects at the window before deciding to go to Kroger. I obtained several witnesses' names and information to cover myself in case this guy was hurt bad.

When the ambulance arrived, the paramedics were not able to revive our unconscious drunk either. They transported him to the hospital. When I got to the hospital, the doctor told me that they had X-rayed the subject and found that he had a fracture on the back of his skull from where he hit the pavement. He did not seem to think it was too serious. I called my sergeant, Sergeant Bob, and told him what had happened. He did not seem to be overly concerned either.

I went ahead and secured warrants on the guy for Simple Assault on me and the Kroger manager, as well as one for Public Drunk. I felt like he should have been charged with Aggravated Assault due to the fact that the rock he was holding would have done a lot of damage. The judge did not see it that way and only issued warrants for Simple Assault, a misdemeanor. These charges would be waiting for him when he was released from the hospital. In reality, however, he was not going to be released from the hospital. I got a call a couple of days later from one of the nurses. She told me that the subject was not responding to treatment and they were going to have a neurologist check him. She was letting me know because the county government was going to be responsible for the man's medical bills and they were getting higher by the day.

When I saw Sergeant Bob, I told him what the nurse had said. He asked me, "What did you do to that guy?" I noticed that he now seemed a little more concerned. He made a few phone calls up the chain of command, letting those above him know about this situation. Somewhere up the chain, someone decided that Internal Affairs should probably look into this. That did not help my state of mind. I was already starting to feel bad for hurting the guy so seriously. Granted, I'm glad he didn't hit me in the face with that one pound rock. If he had, I might be the one in the hospital waiting on the neurologist.

I had only been with the police department a little over a year and had, so far, avoided having to deal with Internal Affairs. I showed up at their office at the appointed time and met with Sergeant Mike, who was going to interview me. He had read my report and had interviewed the witnesses. This made me feel better because I knew that he at least had all the facts in front of him. He asked me a few questions about the incident and about what we did at the scene.

The next thing Sergeant Mike did, though, was to give me an update on the suspect's condition. He told me that the neurologist had diagnosed him with a serious medical condition. The brain had been damaged when his skull smashed into the pavement and he would never fully recover. He would require some type of care for the rest of his life, or as Sergeant Mike so tactfully put it, "He'll need someone to water him and turn him towards the light a couple of times a day."

I was devastated. I had not intended to injure the man. He had tried to punch me and I managed to get him first. I quickly went over the scenario in my mind and really could not think of any other way it could have been handled. That did not make me feel any better, though. Here was a man that I had essentially robbed of the rest of his life. The look on my face must have shown how bad I felt.

Sergeant Mike then reached into a manila folder and pulled out a sheaf of six or seven sheets of paper. He handed it out to me and said, "I want you to read this. It is the suspect's criminal history." As I started to read, I began to feel better. I came to realize that this had been a very dangerous man. He had been arrested on multiple occasions for assaulting police officers, resisting arrest, assault and battery, public drunkenness, as well as many other offenses. The only surprise was why he was not already in jail. Some of the charges had been reduced to less serious ones to dispose of them.

When I finished reading the Criminal History, Sergeant Mike said, "I know you feel bad about this. None of us wants to hurt anyone. But I want you to know something. By taking this guy out, you may have saved another police officer's life. You might have saved a citizen's life. This guy was a powder keg just waiting to explode. Because of your actions, Officer Spell, we do not have to worry about this man anymore. He will never cause anyone another problem." Sergeant Mike's words were exactly what I needed to hear. The cloud lifted off of my mind and I left that interview room knowing that I had done my job and had done it well.

4

Church Burglar

I WAS WORKING ANOTHER winter's night in 1985. It was after midnight and was very cold. There was nothing going on. The police radio was silent. There was little traffic on the road. It was a good night to drink coffee and maybe read the newspaper. It was not to be. The police radio crackled to life and dispatched me and Officer Georgia to a Burglary in Progress at a nearby church. Officer Georgia had been one of my academy mates.

I was close by and was on scene within five minutes. I pulled into the lower parking lot of the Lake Lucerne Baptist Church with my lights off. I intended to park and walk around the church until I found the point of entry. As I got out of my police car and started walking, I could hear voices and yelling coming from the upper parking lot. I ran up there and saw a group of people standing in a circle around four men fighting with another man who was on the ground. Actually, they weren't really fighting him. They were holding him down and punching him every time he tried to get up. One of the punchers was yelling at the man they were holding down and said, "You sacrilegious piece of . . ." The rest was covered by the rest of the crowd chiming in. Someone in the crowd saw me and pointed at the man who was being held down and said, "He's the one, Officer. He's the one who was breaking into the church." This group of people that had apprehended the man were incensed that this fellow had tried to burglarize a place of worship.

One of the onlookers told me that they had all been at the bar directly across the street from the church. They were all drinking and having a good time when they heard several loud crashes and glass breaking across the street at the Baptist Church. They looked out and saw the man they were restraining smash out the light fixture near the front door and then try to force the door open. The witnesses called the police and waited, maintaining a visual on the burglar. The witnesses saw me pull into the lower parking lot, but so did the suspect. He slipped around the far side of the building and might have escaped had not these concerned citizens jumped into action.

Several of them ran across Highway 78 and tackled him so he could not get away. My police car was now parked about one hundred yards away, almost on the other side of the building. The burglar was still re-sisting as the four men held him down. Rather than try and walk him all the way around to my car, it would be much easier to bring my police car up to the upper parking lot.

I said, "Hey, can you guys hold him for a couple more minutes while I go get my police car?"

One of them replied, "No problem, Officer. He's not going anywhere."

By the time I got back with my police car, the suspect had had enough. He was no longer resisting and said, "Please, just take me to jail." I handcuffed him and secured him in my car. I noticed a marble vase lying next to where the burglar had been lying.

One of the witnesses handed me another one and said, "He had this one in his jacket." These marble vases were the kind like you might find flowers in at a cemetery. The weighed a couple of pounds apiece. The suspect also had a plastic beer pitcher that said, "Oliver's" on it. Oliver's was another bar about half a mile up the street.

Officer Georgia had arrived and had checked the outside of the church. She found a screen pried off in the back and some other lights broken out. One of the pastors was called out. After checking the build-ing, he told us that it did not look like the man had managed to get inside. The front door had also been damaged but no entry had been made. The pastor told me he had never seen those two marble vases before. They had not come from the church.

I attempted to interview the suspect. That was a waste of time. He was very intoxicated and nothing he said made any sense. He did seem grateful, though, that I had rescued him from the mob that wanted to pummel him for trying to break into a church. I asked Officer Georgia if she would check the businesses up Hwy 78 back towards Oliver's Bar and see if she could find any other evidence of criminal activity. Within just a few minutes, she returned and told me that our guy had been at the monument company just up from the church. This company made tombstones, memorial plaques and other items, like vases, out of marble. It was obvious that was where he had gotten the vases. The one-man crime spree had also done a substantial amount of damage at the monument company, smashing a number of marble accessories in the parking lot and knocking some of the larger tombstones over.

We were finally able to piece together that this guy had been at Oliver's most of the evening and had had quite a bit to drink. He either did not have a car or was just smart enough not to drive. He lived about a mile away and was walking home. He decided to stop by the monument company to smash some stuff and steal some vases. When he got to the church, he decided that he needed to get inside. Maybe he needed a place to pray, but I doubt it. He was probably hoping to find something else to steal or vandalize. For his trouble, he was charged with two felonies and a misdemeanor. This was a wonderful instance of citizens being willing to get involved and not allow a criminal to escape.

5

Drunk Prowler

IT WAS ALMOST 6:00 in the morning. The next shift would be coming on at 6:30 and then I could go home and go to bed. Instead, the call from radio meant that I would not be getting to bed on time: "Be enroute to a Prowler attempting to force entry at a residence. The description of the perp is a black male wearing a black jacket." I hurried to the address that dispatch sent me to. A big, fat white male met me at the door wearing nothing but his white Fruit of the Looms. I could see his wife holding a baby standing behind him. I thought, *You could have at least put some pants on!*

As he told me what had happened, however, it was clear that this poor fellow had just been awakened by the black guy banging on his front door. He said, "Officer, I heard this banging on the door so I went to see what the commotion was about."

I said, "You didn't open the door, did you?"

He said, "Well, I just opened it a crack and this black guy shoved his way into my house. I didn't know what he wanted so I shoved him back out and slammed the door. That is when I called the police."

While I was talking to Mr. Fruit of the Loom, I heard the dispatcher advise that the same male was trying to get into another home on the next street over. I quickly drove to that location. A lady met me at the door. She was clearly shaken. I asked her what had happened. Her story was almost identical as the first one. "I heard someone pounding on my door and went to see who it was."

I asked her the same question, "You didn't open the door, did you?" She said that she had opened the door but she had been holding her poodle at the time. When the suspect tried to shove his way into her house, the poodle started barking and lunged for the intruder. This was enough for the guy to call it quits at this house. He did not want to have to deal with a vicious poodle. The prowler ran away.

As I was talking with this lady, another call came over the police radio in reference to an intruder breaking into another home. This one was also in the same neighborhood, on the street behind the one I was on. I drove over there and found that the suspect had gone around behind this house. The front door was not working out so good for him so he decided to try the back. He had walked up on the deck. This home had beautiful double French doors leading into the house from the deck. The prowler grabbed a piece of firewood that was laying there and smashed open one of the doors.

The homeowner told me that he awakened immediately when he heard the glass shatter and he could hear someone walking in his house. The homeowner had yelled out, "I have a shotgun and I'll kill you." He then heard the sound of someone running out and across the deck. When he checked, he found that the suspect had fled.

"It's a good thing he did, Officer, or I would have shot him," the victim told me. I assured the man that I understood completely and he was certainly entitled to protect his family and his home.

At that moment, another call came from Police Dispatch of a suspicious person pounding on someone else's door. This call was also in the immediate area, just down the street. When I got there, the suspect had again already fled. The lady at this house said she had been awakened by someone pounding on the door. She was not expecting any visitors at 6:15 in the morning so she immediately called the police.

How long are we going to have to chase this guy? I wondered. *He will eventually get into a house and hurt someone or he is going to get shot.* As it turned out, the prowler's night on the town was about to come to an end.

While I was talking with this lady, one more 911 call came in of a black male attempting to get into another house a few streets over. This time, when I pulled up in my cruiser, I saw a black male wearing a black jacket pounding on the front door of the residence. The homeowners were watching him from their living room window, still on the phone with the 911 operator.

I approached the suspect with my service revolver drawn and ordered him to the ground. He complied and I was able to get him handcuffed, searched and in my police car. When the man realized that he was under arrest, he started crying like a baby. He bawled for several minutes. It didn't take long to realize that he was very intoxicated.

After he quit crying, I interviewed this intoxicated man, Lamont, and was able to piece his sad story together. Lamont was from Columbus, Georgia. That is about three hours South of where he ended up. He and several of his friends had come to Atlanta to party. After everybody got good and drunk, they were trying to find their way back to Columbus but got very lost. Lamont told me that at some point, his friends got mad at him and dumped him out in Snellville, Georgia. He wasn't sure what he did to make them mad. "I don't remember a whole lot," he said.

What he did remember, though, was that he did not know where he was and was trying to get to a phone. "I didn't mean no harm," he assured me. I am sure that made everyone that he had terrorized that morning feel a lot better!

The Magistrate Judge gave me three warrants, a felony and two misdemeanors. I wanted three felonies but the Judge would not give them to me. The felony was for the house that he had smashed the French door open. The two misdemeanors were for the two houses that he shoved his way into when the people had opened the door.

When this case went to trial, I got pretty disgusted with the way the prosecution handled it. The District Attorney's Office (they prosecute felony cases) decided that the felony Burglary charge that I had made was not a good charge. Try telling that to the man whose house was broken into. The DA's Office dropped the charge down to a misdemeanor Criminal Trespass charge like the other two.

Now the case was going to be handled by the Solicitor's Office (they prosecute misdemeanors). They decided to drop the two cases where the guy shoved his way into people's homes. "You can't prove criminal intent to commit a crime," one the Assistant Solicitors told me.

In the end, they let Lamont plead guilty to the other Criminal Trespass charge in which he violently broke into the house. The sentence was twelve months of non-reporting probation and a two hundred dollar fine. Maybe the next time this perp gets drunk and lost at 6:00 in the morning, he will wind up at one of the Assistant DA's or Assistant Solicitor's houses. Or better yet, maybe he will meet an armed homeowner who is not afraid to do what it takes to protect his family.

6

My First Homicide

EVERY OFFICER REMEMBERS THEIR first Homicide investigation. Mine started with a call to a home in the black section of the little town of Buford. The call came out as an Assault. The dispatcher merely told me that one brother had assaulted another. She also told me that there were no back up units available. It was almost 11:00 at night and I had just started my shift when the 911 call came in to the police department.

When I pulled up to the house, I noticed several people milling about in the front yard. I asked them what happened. One of men said, "He's in the house and he needs an ambulance. Freddie's hurt bad."

I asked who hurt him and was told, "His brother, George, did it, but he done left." I went into the house and found about twenty people standing around, all of them looking very concerned. Someone pointed to the couch. I saw a male that turned out to be Freddie lying on the couch. A young woman named Mary was cradling his head in her lap. She was holding a rag to the side of Freddie's head.

I thought, *Freddie must have gotten beat up pretty good.* When I looked closer, however, I realized that this was much more serious. This was not just the case of two brothers fighting. When I looked at Freddie's face, I saw that it was covered with blood. He was bleeding from the right ear and his right eye was bulging unnaturally out of its socket. Mary pulled the rag back so I could see the wound to the side of Freddie's head. There was a long, deep wound running from just behind his right eye to above his right ear. The gash was about five inches long and deep.

I asked Mary if she knew what had happened. She told me that she was the cousin of the two men and lived one street over. Mary then said, "George hit Freddie in the head with an axe while he was sleeping."

An axe? I wondered. *I thought people only got hit with axes in movies. Wow!*

At this point, the paramedics arrived. They took one look at the severity of the wound and quickly loaded Freddie into the ambulance for transport to the hospital. He was still alive but I was doubtful that he would be for long. I notified my supervisor, Sergeant Larry, of the severity of the incident. Detectives and the CSI Unit were also requested.

Freddie and George were both in their forties but still lived with their parents. Their father, Johnny, told me that the two brothers had been arguing earlier in the evening. Both brothers had been drinking heavily. Freddie had pulled a .22 rifle on George and threatened to kill him with it. Johnny took George and they left the house so that both brothers could cool off. They were gone for over an hour and when they came home Freddie was sleeping, or passed out, on the couch.

Johnny had then gone into his room to go to bed and thought that George had done the same thing. A little while later, however, Johnny said that George came into his bedroom and said, "Daddy, you need to call the police to come get me, 'cause I just killed Freddie." George then left the house, got in his car, and drove away. When Johnny checked and found his other son with his head gashed open and unconscious on the couch, he called 911.

With all of the family members at the house, this was a very difficult crime scene to control. Normally, we would just order everyone out and lock it down until CSI had processed it. There were two problems with that here. First of all, it was January so it was cold outside. The second problem, though, was that the two brothers' mother, Johnny's wife, was an invalid and was bedridden. She could not be moved and someone had to stay with her. I got rid of as many people as I could but there were still a number of people in the house.

I still had not seen the axe that had been used in the assault. I mentioned this to Mary. She said, "I know where the axe is." Without another word, she stepped into a bedroom and came back out with a full size axe. It looked like the blade had been recently wiped off. Mary motioned to the room that she had just come out of and said, "That is George's room. The axe was on the bed."

Normally, the detectives would have secured a Search Warrant to go into George's room to find the weapon. Mary, however, was not subject to the Search and Seizure Rules that police officers are. With all of the people milling about the house, it would have been very easy for that axe to "disappear." With Mary's help, I was able to secure it for the detectives. I took it outside and put it in the trunk of my police car for the time being.

While still waiting on the investigators to get there, another family member showed up at the house. She was Mary's mother and the boys' aunt and lived on the next street over. She said that George had just driven up to her house and had told her, "I killed Freddie and I know the police are going to be looking for me." He then drove off. At this same time, several of the people in the front yard started yelling that George had just driven by.

Another officer, Officer Randy, one of my academy mates, had come to the scene to help me try and maintain some order. When it became obvious that George was still in the neighborhood, Randy started to go looking for him. As he was about to get into his police car, George came driving by again. Randy just motioned for him to pull over, which he did. He actually stopped in his own driveway. He was quickly taken into custody and secured in one of the police cars.

While we were arresting George, Randy and I both observed that he was very, very drunk. Randy went ahead and charged him with Driving Under the Influence and several other traffic charges. He registered .30 grams on the intoximeter. That is a staggering number. It is over three times the legal limit. Randy would transport George to the Headquarters where the detectives could interview him. I would stay at the crime scene until CSI was finished processing it and the investigators that we were on scene had finished interviewing witnesses.

On the way to the Headquarters, George told Officer Randy, "Freddie was drunk and had been threatening me and Daddy with that gun. When he come at me with the gun, I hit him with the ax." George was initially booked on Aggravated Battery, as well as the traffic charges.

Freddie managed to hold on to life for about three weeks before he died. George's charges were then upgraded to Murder. When his case went to trial a few months later, his lawyer said that he was going to plead that he acted in self defense. All the evidence, however, indicated that Freddie was asleep on the couch when George hit him with the ax. In the end, just before the trial started, George pleaded guilty to Murder. He received a Life Sentence, which is a bit deceiving. George was eligible for Parole after seven years. In reality, he served less than ten years, and as far as I know is back home in Buford, minus his brother.

7

A Long Foot Chase

Sometimes, what you see is not what you get. Looks can be deceiving. I was patrolling the small town of Grayson. They do not have their own police department so the county provides coverage for them. This took place in November of 1984 around 11:15 at night. I saw a gray 1975 Buick Apollo parked on the shoulder of Highway 20. It looked like they were broken down. I could see that the right rear tire was flat and almost off the rim. I advised the dispatcher that I would be out on a stranded motorist. I gave her my location and the tag number of the car and activated my blue light.

As I approached the Apollo to see what I could do to help, I noticed that the driver was attempting to move the vehicle. I could see sparks coming from the rim of the flat tire but then I saw that the car was hung up on the curb. Before I could get up to the Buick, however, the driver's door flew open and a white male bailed out or the driver's seat and started running. It's been said that police officers are like Labrador Retrievers. We will chase anything that runs. There is some truth to that. The problem was I had told the dispatcher I was out on a stranded motorist, not in a foot chase. We did not have walkie talkies yet. I hesitated for a moment trying to decide what to do: go back to my patrol car, update radio and request backup or purse the fleeing man. I chose to chase the guy that was trying to get away.

By now, he had about a twenty five yard head start on me. He was running across the parking lot of the First Baptist Church of Grayson. I never have been a great runner but I was only 22 years old at the time and was in pretty good shape. The guy I was chasing was a good sized guy. He was about six foot and weighed at least two hundred pounds. I should have been able to catch him but fear and adrenaline sometimes give people that extra little push. I was yelling at the subject to stop but he just kept running.

We ran behind a house that was the church parsonage, continued behind the church and then back in the direction that we had come. He was trying to get back to his car. After almost two hundred yards, I was starting to close the distance. I was only about ten yards behind him when he turned around to see where I was. That was his undoing. He lost his balance and fell hard to the ground, face first. Before he could try and get back up I dove on top of him. He was about my age and it was clear he was not going to go without a fight. The problem was the long run had winded us both. We just lay there for a few minutes trying to catch our breath. The guy, who turned out to be twenty two years old as well, then started trying buck me off.

I could smell the alcohol on the guy and now realized that he had run because he was driving under the influence and had wrecked his car. I needed to get him handcuffed but he was starting to get his wind back. I managed to get his left wrist handcuffed but his right arm was under him and he kept trying to throw his right elbow at me. Every time he did I punched him in the back. At the time, we carried very cheap, very flimsy flashlights. I had left my nightstick in the car. After all, this was only a stranded motorist. After struggling unsuccessfully for several minutes to get his right hand cuffed, I swung my flashlight at the suspect's head. Instead of stunning the suspect like I had hoped, my cheap flashlight disintegrated into several pieces all over the ground.

The drunk guy that I was wrestling with said, "Ouch! Is that all you've got?"

Now I did not have a flashlight and I was fighting this guy in the dark. I started punching his back and right shoulder in an effort to make him give me his right hand so I could handcuff him. It was not having any effect. Finally, I reached behind me and grabbed the drunk's testicles. I started to squeeze. He began to scream and curse me with everything he had.

"Give me your right hand," I ordered.

His level of profanity only increased. I continued to squeeze his testicles until the pain was too much for him, even in his highly intoxicated state. He pulled his right out from underneath him and put it behind his back. I quickly got him handcuffed and searched for weapons.

As I was trying to get the subject to his feet, (no easy task considering his size, level of intoxication, and handcuffs) a man came running up and said, "Officer, are you okay? I saw your car down there and somebody else driving by had seen you run up here. I wanted to make sure you were alright."

I asked him to help me get the drunk to his feet. The helpful citizen did and then helped me walk him the one hundred plus yards back to the cars we had left behind. On the walk back, the drunk continued to resist and try to pull away, using many colorful phrases and expletives. My helpful citizen appeared shocked. He told the guy, "Listen here, buddy. You need to watch your mouth!"

By the time we got to the cars, Officer John had shown up. When I had not reported back into the dispatcher within five minutes as we are required to do, she had sent another officer to check on me. I thanked the citizen for stopping to help me and shook his hand. He did not have to get involved but he felt like it was the right thing to do.

My arrestee was less than enthusiastic about getting into a police car and Officer John and I had to force him in. A computer check showed that he was a Habitual Traffic Offender which meant that his driver's license had been revoked for five years and it was a felony for him to be driving. He was charged with that, as well as Driving Under the Influence and Resisting Arrest. Our investigation discovered that the subject had driven off the road just up from where we were and had hit a "School Bus Entering the Highway" sign and knocked it over. He then swerved back onto the road and continued to where I had found him. He had hit the curb and destroyed both of his passenger side tires, actually knocking them loose from the rims. With my charges and the suspect's previous criminal history, he spent almost a year in jail.

8

Shots Fired

IT WAS ANOTHER COLD winter's night in 1988. Nothing was going on anywhere in the county. It was another good night to drink coffee and stay in my warm car. About two in the morning, however, the radio crackled to life. "Be enroute to shots fired. The caller heard multiple shots near her residence," the dispatcher advised.

The address was in a set of duplexes just outside the city of Lilburn. Officer Rick, one of my academy mates, cleared with me. While this sounded like a good call, most of the time "shots fired" calls turned out to be nothing. Usually, you would drive around the area never hearing anything. Seldom were you ever given a specific location, just a general area. If you happened to locate it, it often just turned out to be kids setting off fireworks.

On this call, though, we were given a specific address. It did not say whether it was on the "A" side or the "B" side of the duplex, but it was better than a general area. Rick and I parked across the street from the location and got out. The building was dark and it appeared that everyone was asleep. We decided to walk around behind the duplex and see if there was anybody back there. It is always embarrassing when officers leave a call without checking things thoroughly enough and it comes out later that they missed a body lying in the backyard. Believe it or not, that does happen.

When we got to the back of the building, we did not see or hear everything. There were no lights on back there and it was very dark. We illuminated the yard with our flashlights and did not see anyone lurking in the shadows. We were getting ready to walk back around to the front when we heard voices. A window was open near where we were standing and we could hear some people speaking Spanish inside the duplex. There was the sound of a pistol action being worked and then we heard

29

footsteps approaching the window. Rick and I pressed ourselves flat against the wall. An arm was suddenly thrust out of the open window and was holding a pistol. It fired seven shots towards the woods behind the building. Just before the shots went off, I caught a glimpse of a single bed next to the window. We instinctively dropped to the ground and crawled around the corner of the building. We then got up and ran back to our police cars.

Both of us were a little excited. It is not every day that you get shot at. Okay, we weren't really shot at. I don't think the Hispanic guy with the gun even knew we were out there. But we were only about ten feet away from the window when the guy let loose with the pistol and it was a bit unnerving. I got on the radio and called for backup. When we got some more officers there, we were going to go and arrest this clown for shooting out of his window. For starters, it is illegal to discharge a firearm in a residential area. There were other possible charges that we would explore after we got the perp in custody.

Within just a few minutes, we had several more officers out with us. Lieutenant Chris was running the shift that night without any Sergeants. When he got there, Rick and I briefed him on what we had. "I'm not sure which side of the duplex the shooter is in," I told him. Rick and I both thought it was the "A" side and we told Lieutenant Chris so.

The Lieutenant quickly took charge. He sent a couple of officers to watch the rear. The Lieutenant, Rick, me, and another officer went to the front door of apartment "A" and knocked. A middle-aged Hispanic man came to the door in his underwear. He appeared to have just woken up.

Lieutenant Chris yelled at the guy, "Were you shooting? Where is the pistol? El pistol?"

The man appeared apologetic and said, "No English."

Unfazed, the Lieutenant just got louder with his English, "Where is the pistol? If you don't tell us where the gun is, we are going to have you deported!" The poor guy only looked more confused.

I tried a different strategy. I motioned inside and asked if we could come in. He very kindly let us in, but in retrospect, there wasn't much chance of him refusing. I was holding my shotgun and the other officers had their revolvers out. When we stepped inside, I saw a door against the far wall. That was the only room where the shots could have come from. I told the Lieutenant, "That's the room."

He knocked on the door. The man tried to tell us something but none of us spoke Spanish. We did not get any response to the knocking, so we tried the knob. It was locked. The Lieutenant, without hesitation, kicked the door open. When I saw the baby bed next to the window, I realized that I had screwed up. That wasn't the bed that I had seen through the window when we were outside. Fortunately, the baby slept through the whole fracas. I told the Lieutenant and the others that we needed to be on the other side of the duplex in the "B" apartment.

We started for the other apartment. I wasn't sure how the Lieutenant was going to handle the fact that we were in the wrong apartment or that we had kicked in the wrong door, but he did not seem particularly concerned. He told the Hispanic guy, "Alright, we are leaving but don't make us come back over here!"

When we knocked on the other door at side "B", a teenaged Hispanic girl opened it. She did not seem surprised to see us and let us into the apartment. She spoke some English and when we asked who was shooting, she motioned with her head towards a closed door off of the living room. Maybe she had heard what had happened next door because she walked over and opened the bedroom door for us and stepped back.

This was the right bedroom. I recognized the bed under the window. Only now, there was a guy laying in it pretending to be asleep. He had the covers pulled up to his chin and we could not see his hands. He could be pointing the pistol at us and we would not even know it until he started shooting. All four of us started yelling at him to let us see his hands. He continued to pretend that he was asleep.

There were a couple of other bedrooms in the duplex and we had managed to wake up the other ten people that lived there. Several men, women, and children came out of these rooms rubbing their eyes. The teenage girl briefed them in Spanish on what was going on. They started yelling at the guy in the bed, too. I don't know what they were saying, but it was clear they were not happy with this clown.

I guess he thought that if he ignored us, we would just go away. He kept acting like he was asleep. Lieutenant Chris then holstered his gun and ran across the room and dove on top of the "sleeper." This is not a move that they teach in the police academy. Lieutenant Chris had always been a little unorthodox, though. The problem with this tactic was that if the man did have the gun under the covers with him, he could very easily shoot the Lieutenant. The end result of that, of course, would be that the other three of us would kill the guy. I really thought that the Lieutenant was about to get shot, so I stepped sideways to get a better angle at the guy's head. As I did, I racked a round into the chamber of my shotgun and the other two officers positioned themselves to shoot as well.

At the sound of the shotgun being racked, the "sleeper" woke up and looked down the barrel of the 12 gauge shotgun. Lieutenant Chris pulled the sheet off of the man and we saw that his hands were empty. The Lieutenant turned him over and we handcuffed him. By now, we could all smell the alcohol and understood that our new friend, Jose, was very drunk. We asked him where the pistol was. He mumbled some slurred words in Spanish that none of us understood.

Officer Rick asked the girl where the gun was. She asked the drunk guy in Spanish. She then translated his answer for us, "He say he no have a gun."

I asked her if he was the one who was shooting a gun out the window. She said that he was. "Ok, so where is the gun?" I asked.

She said, "I don't know. Maybe he hide it." That was all we needed to hear. We searched the bedroom thoroughly. We checked the bed, including flipping the mattress. We looked in the closet and the dresser. We searched every nook and corner and came up empty.

I told the girl who was helping us, "Check with everyone else and see if they know where the pistol is. As soon as we get the gun, we are taking Jose to jail and we will be leaving. If no one helps us, we will search the rest of the apartment and it will not be pretty."

She quickly translated this to the rest of the occupants. Another teenage girl walked up to me and led me back into the living room and pointed at the television. I really wasn't in the mood to watch TV and wasn't sure what she meant. She then walked over to the television and removed the back panel. She just pulled it right off. I looked inside and there was the pistol that Officer Rick and I had seen Jose shooting out the back window.

We thanked the girls for helping us. Their cooperation had really sped things up. We packed Jose in the back of my police car and I took him to jail. He was charged with Discharging a Firearm within 500 Feet of a Residence and Reckless Conduct. His pistol was placed in the Evidence Room and he probably never saw it again.

9

Crazy Lady with a Gun

THIS CHAPTER DETAILS AN instance in which I had to deal with someone with mental issues. It is not my purpose to offend anyone if they have family members that have been diagnosed with some form of mental illness. In my line of work, officers encounter mentally ill people everyday and handle them with compassion and care. Back at the precinct, however, at the end of shift, these stories often provide great stress relieving laughter as they are shared.

Mrs. Johnson could have been anyone's grandmother. She was in her late 70s. She was only about five feet tall and weighed about one hundred pounds. Her gray hair always looked like she had just come from the beauty parlor and she was always well dressed. All of the officers at the Southside Precinct got to know Mrs. Johnson or knew of her. We knew that her husband had died several years earlier and she lived by herself. She would call in about once or twice a month complaining that her neighbors were in her attic spying on her. When asked how she knew they were in her attic, Mrs. Johnson would say, "Why, I can hear them, of course!" That was a surprise because she was very hard of hearing. We had to yell to make ourselves heard whenever we were at her house. Even then, she often misunderstood what we were saying.

When Mrs. Johnson got a security system installed, the calls to her house increased to several times a week. She had no idea how to use her alarm system and set it off every few days. It got to the point that when we got the burglar alarm call at her house, we would go out there and walk around the house and leave. We seldom tried to make contact with Mrs. Johnson for two reasons. First of all, she could not hear the doorbell or the knocking on her door. And second, none of us wanted to have to hear the saga of her neighbors jumping around in her attic.

After a few months of this, we got some ominous news. Mrs. Johnson had acquired a gun. Someone, probably a family member had given her a revolver for personal protection. Now, I'm a Second Amendment guy all the way. I believe that people should be able to have guns to protect themselves. I just don't think crazy people should have guns.

With Mrs. Johnson now being armed, this changed the entire dynamic of officers responding to her house. Now, when we responded to an alarm call, we always tried to alert her that we were there. We didn't want to startle Mrs. Johnson and put us in a position where we would have her shooting at us. The problem, however, like I mentioned earlier, was that she was hard of hearing and usually did not hear us at her door.

One of the officers at Southside did a little research and discovered that Mrs. Johnson had a daughter that lived nearby. The next time that I got an alarm call, I had our dispatcher call the daughter and meet with me at her mother's house. Debbie was a very nice lady in her late 40s. I laid the scenario out for Debbie. I requested that she get her mother's gun out of the house and also to consider disconnecting the security system. Debbie agreed to take the gun to her house. As for the security system, she was going to check with the company and see if they would only dispatch for medical calls. I could live with that.

Debbie and I then went up to the house. Debbie had a key and let us inside. I was pretty nervous because I did not want to startle this deaf, armed, little old lady, who was already imagining people were in her house. Debbie found her mom in the kitchen. She was holding her revolver at her side, but when she saw her daughter, she laid the gun down. I grabbed it and unloaded it. It was an old Smith & Wesson .32 revolver. It didn't look like it would even fire but I wasn't taking any chances. I put the bullets in my pocket.

Mrs. Johnson looked relieved to see me. "I am so glad you are here, Officer. They are back," she said.

"Who is back, ma'am?" I asked knowing full well what she was talking about. She said, "Come on. I'll show you." She walked down the hallway and stopped underneath her attic door, and pointed up. "They are up there. They don't think I know, but I know," she said.

I looked up at the attic and saw that she had had someone equip it with padlocks, two of them. My curiosity got the best of me. "Mrs.

Johnson, how are they getting into your attic? You have it locked up pretty tight."

She lowered her voice in a conspiratorial tone and said, "They come in through the vents on the roof."

That was a revelation. I asked her, raising my voice so she could hear me, "How do they get through those vents, Mrs. Johnson? They are really small."

The plot got thicker. She told me, "They work for the FBI and they must have some kind of machine that shrinks them so they can slip through."

It was all becoming clear now. This was just a small part of a much bigger government conspiracy. I was in this far. I might as well keep going. "So, Mrs. Johnson, why does the FBI have people watching you?"

She chuckled and said, "They think I am a spy."

I took a shot in the dark. "I think I can solve your problem, Mrs. Johnson." Her eyes lit up in anticipation. I continued, "How about if I call the FBI and tell them to pull their people out and quit watching you. I will them that I have talked to you and it is obvious that you are not a spy."

She seemed genuinely relieved. "Would you do that for me?" she asked. I assured her that I would and started moving towards the door in an effort to get away from the madness.

Mrs. Johnson's daughter walked outside with me. She said, "Thank you for humoring my mother. I know you have better things to do than to talk to crazy old women." I assured her that it was just part of the job. Then things got really bizarre.

Debbie said, "That is a new one. I have never heard of people climbing down into the attic through the vents on the roof."

We both chuckled. Then I saw the same weird look come into her eyes that I had just see in her mother's. Debbie said, "At my house, the little men come in through my mirror."

I thought she was kidding, but after a moment, I realized that she was completely serious and was waiting for me to say something. What do you say to that? "Wow! That is interesting," was about the best I could do.

Debbie said, "I know it sounds weird, but they visit me about once a week."

This was feeling pretty creepy. "Who are they?" I asked.

She answered me slowly, "I'm not really sure. They are about two feet tall. They climb out of the mirror into my bedroom and play in the floor. After a little while, they climb back into the mirror and leave."

Did I really want Debbie to have her mom's gun? At this point, I really didn't care. I just wanted to leave and get away from these two as quickly as I could. I still had the bullets to the gun in my pocket, so I told Debbie I hoped everything worked out OK for her and the little guys. I told Debbie that I had another call I had to get to, got in my police car and left.

As it turned out, I never responded to another call at Mrs. Johnson's house. She believed that I had pulled some strings with the FBI and had those people leave her attic for good. As for Debbie, she is probably still enjoying her weekly show put on by the little men from inside her mirror.

10

Introduction to Domestic Calls

DOMESTIC CALLS CAN COME in many different forms. Most of the time, they are between a husband and wife or a boyfriend and girl-friend. They can also be between parents and children, brothers and sisters, in-laws, roommates, neighbors or just about any other combination that one could imagine. Some officers don't like handling domestic calls. I know they can be dangerous, but they are also highly entertaining. The fact of the matter is: you just can't make some of this stuff up!

While one of my own daughters was going through a semi-rebellious period, I handled a domestic call between a woman and her fifteen year old daughter. This girl was climbing out her window at night (she lived on the second floor), dropping to the ground and then going to meet her boyfriend. She was active sexually, smoking, drinking, and admitted to using marijuana. When I got to the house, it was about 5:00 in the morning and the young lady had just crawled back into her room, where her mother was waiting for her.

The confrontation had been heated, with a lot of yelling and throwing things at each other. When I got there, the other officer and I were able to get everything calmed down. We recommended family counseling, but I could see by the look in their eyes that that was probably not going to happen. The young girl told me, "She can't control my life. If I want to go sleep with my boyfriend, she can't stop me."

What can you say to that? Eventually, she would end up pregnant or cross the line and end up in jail or both. For now, however, things were somewhat peaceful again and the other officer and I prepared to leave.

I could hear the mother tell her daughter as we walked out the door, "Well, let me tell you one thing: just as soon as your daddy gets out of prison, you are going to live with him!"

As I got back in my police car, I realized that my own situation with my daughter was not even close to being as bad as what I had witnessed. I thanked God for the perspective that He had given me. Both of my daughters are grown now, married, serving God and leading productive lives. What more can any parent ask for?

On another night, I got a call to a residence in a neighborhood in Buford. This was a "regular" address, meaning we were out there once a week or so. We seldom had to arrest anyone here. Usually, it was just a lot of yelling and screaming. The main issue was that both the husband and the wife had substance abuse issues, or in layman's terms, they were drug addicts.

On this particular night, when I got to the house, the wife, Patti, was there by herself. I asked her what was going on. She said, "Jeff spent all of the grocery money on crack cocaine, and the worst part is that he smoked it all. He didn't save any crack for me." What can you possibly say to someone with that kind of a problem?

Other domestic calls are more violent. In August of 1995, I was dispatched to a Man Beating a Woman domestic call at an address in Buford. I pulled up to the house at 11:20 in the evening. A woman met me in the front yard. She was out of breath as she told me, "He's beating her. Please make him stop."

The home was a duplex. The lady who had flagged me down lived on one side but had been awakened by screaming, yelling, and something (or someone), being slammed into the wall separating the two sides of the duplex. From outside in the front yard, I could hear a woman's voice inside the house pleading, "Please stop!"

An angry male's voice replied, "You just don't know when to quit, do you?"

The neighbor that I had first spoken to told me she had a key and would let me in. As she was unlocking the door, I heard what sounded like someone being thrown into a wall. When the door opened, I saw a man holding a woman down on a couch. She was shielding her face with her hands.

As I stepped into the room, the man saw that the police were there, released the woman and sat down in a chair. I could see that the woman's lower lip was swollen and bloody. She had a lump under her eye from where it looked like she had been punched. Another officer arrived and I spoke to the woman, Cindy, privately in the next room. She told me that she and her boyfriend, Larry, had been drinking all evening and then they had started arguing. He had been slapping her in the face, pulling her hair, and throwing her around their apartment for the last two hours. I could also see where Larry had damaged the apartment. There were several holes that he had punched in the walls and bedroom door.

When I walked back into the living room where Larry was being interviewed by the other officer, I saw their small dog walk over to Larry to be petted. Evidently, Larry was mad at everyone that night because he picked up the dog and threw it across the room. Fortunately, the dog wasn't hurt. Larry was arrested on Domestic Violence charges even as Cindy was begging me not to lock him up. A couple of weeks later, I saw Larry and Cindy walking down the street together, arm in arm. Isn't love grand? I bet even the dog forgave Larry.

Recruit Paul, who I was training at the time, and I responded to a home on an Aggravated Domestic call in December of 2002 at 3:00 in the morning. Ronald met us at the street. He said, "I came over here to get my wife. She is in another man's house and in his bed, so I came to get her and bring her home. She didn't want to come with me so I gave her a good spanking. I wore her butt out! How would you like it if you found your wife in another man's bed?"

I could see that Ronald's hand was bleeding. I asked him how he got cut. He said he cut himself while he was spanking his wife. We could smell alcohol on Ronald's breath. He told us that he had been drinking earlier.

I left Recruit Paul outside with Ronald and went into the house to talk to Susan, his wife. She said that she and Ronald had gone out to a bar earlier and they had both been drinking. Ronald thought that Susan was talking to some other men at the bar and they started arguing. When he started to grab her and get physical, Susan called a mutual male friend, Steve, and asked if she could sleep on his couch. Steve agreed to let her sleep on his couch. Susan then left Ronald at the bar and retreated to Steve's house.

While I was talking to Susan, we were standing in Steve's living room. The couch had a blanket and pillows on it. She motioned to it and said that that was where she had been sleeping when Ronald had come to get her. She said, "I was sleeping. I got woke up when Ronald started yelling and beating my butt. He just would not stop hitting me on the bottom. He knocked me off the couch and when I got up, he started hitting me again. He hit me so hard he split one of his fingers."

Susan pointed to the blood that was splattered on the sofa and the rug. She had welts and bruises on her hips. She said, "I'm not going home with him. He is acting crazy and I am scared of him."

Steve, whose house we were in, was not much help as a witness. He said, "I didn't see anything. I could hear Ron yelling, but I figured it was none of my business so I just stayed in my bedroom. They are both my friends and I didn't want to interfere in their argument."

When we placed Ronald under arrest for Domestic Violence, he was incredulous. "You guys can't be serious! I only beat her on the butt. I just spanked her! I was the one who called you guys. This just isn't right! Can't a guy spank his wife when she gets out of line?"

I think he started to understand the gravity of his situation when the big door slammed shut on the holding cell at the jail. These next few chapters are a sampling of some of the best and worst domestic calls that I have encountered throughout my career.

11

Fighting with Her Mother-in-Law

OFFICER CHRIS AND I were dispatched to an Aggravated Domestic involving a woman who was threatening suicide and who had also said she was going to kill her husband and children. This call occurred in March of 2002 at around 11:30 PM. I got to the house first and was met at the street by a couple, Homer and Peggy, who appeared to be in their 50s. They told me that their son and his family lived there. The problem was with their daughter-in-law, Deborah. "She is going crazy and trying to fight with everybody," Homer said, holding his granddaughter who looked to be about six.

This call took place in a rural area near Grayson and the house sat off the road about 100 yards. I had stopped at the bottom of the driveway and could hear what sounded like a woman yelling and screaming inside the house. Peggy said, "Please, you've got to do something."

I assured that we would as soon as my backup officer got there. I knew he was only a couple of minutes behind me. There have been many times in my career where I have had to handle calls like this one without backup, but it was never by choice. It is always preferable to have another officer or two with you when dealing with volatile situations like this one.

When Peggy saw that I was not going to rush headlong into the house, she turned around and walked quickly up to the house where the screaming was coming from and went in. Whatever she was trying to accomplish did not seem to be working, because after she went in the yelling and screaming only intensified. I could not hear everything that was being said, but I could pick out an occasional profanity and it was clear that the woman who was doing the yelling was not happy.

I could see headlights down the road. I knew that it was Officer Chris. I told Homer that as soon as he got here, we would go in and deal with the situation. Well, that was not good enough for him either. I guess he felt that he needed to go save his overly zealous wife. He rushed back up the hill, still carrying his granddaughter and went into the house.

When Chris pulled up, I briefed him on what little I knew. We both approached the house where Deborah was still screaming and cursing at the top of her lungs. As we got to the front door, Homer came out and said, "My wife is cut. Deborah cut her across the face with a knife."

About that time, Peggy came stumbling out of the house. Her face was covered with blood and she appeared to be bleeding from several locations on her head and face. I thought, *A lot of good you did. You are lucky she did not kill you.* We called for an ambulance and asked her what had happened. She said, "Deborah attacked me and hit me in the face with the telephone."

Chris and I entered the house. We found Deborah in a bedroom yelling into the phone. She had actually just called 911. We got her to put the phone down and asked her what had happened. She said, "Everybody is ganging up on me and they won't let me take my medicine."

She sounded like she had had plenty of medicine. Her speech was slurred and she was unsteady on her feet. She kept saying that she needed her medicine. I asked her what happened to Peggy. Deborah said, "She grabbed me by the arm and told me to calm down. She would not let me go so I hit her in the face with the television remote. I just kept hitting her until she let me go."

We placed Deborah under arrest for Battery. Deborah started screaming profanities at Chris and I, Peggy, and the rest of her family. She yelled and ranted as we escorted her out to my police car. In classic victim fashion, Peggy asked us not to arrest her. "That will only make her mad," she said.

I told Peggy, "She just beat you up and cut your head open with a TV remote control. I think she is already pretty mad." I asked her how she expected us to handle the situation. Deborah appeared to be intoxicated and under the influence of some type of pain pills so it wasn't like we were going to be able to talk with her. Peggy evidently just wanted us to "talk with her and get her calmed down." She would have plenty of time to calm down at the jail.

When this case went to trial, the family requested and got the charges against Deborah dropped. Some officers might take this personally. I don't. We did what we had to do that night to protect the rest of the family from a violent, unstable, and intoxicated family member. Hopefully, they were able to get her some help because the next time she might really use a knife instead of a remote control to do her damage.

12

Fight with an Army Ranger

The call from the dispatcher got my adrenaline pumping. "Be enroute to an Aggravated Domestic Dispute. A father and son are fighting in the front yard. Both subjects have been drinking. The son is armed with a knife. No units are available for backup." Dispatch provided the address and I was on my way. Some officers don't like handling domestic calls. I have always enjoyed them just because you never know what to expect. Are you going to be able to calm the situation down? Is it going to turn into a violent encounter? My police department has a very good Domestic Violence Policy. Officers are required to make arrests in certain situations, mainly where one family member has assaulted and injured another. I had the feeling driving to this call, that this would not be one in which you could just calm things down and leave. I turned out to be right.

Aggravated domestic calls are not the type of call that officers normally handle on their own. This is a priority call and there should be a minimum of two officers responding. This one was intensified even more by the fact that one of the people involved was armed with a knife. Early in my career, however, we really did not have a choice. We just did not have the number of officers that we do now. There were some nights in which we would have six to eight officers covering the entire county. In 2010, our slowest precincts now run at least that number of cars a shift. When you multiply that by five precincts, we now run over fifty cars during the third shift for the entire county. That only counts zone cars, though, and when you throw in officers assigned to Special Operations and other miscellaneous officers, there could be close to one hundred officers available if needed. But not back then. You just got used to handling bad calls by yourself. If you had a backup, you considered yourself fortunate.

The house that I was going to had a big front yard and a fairly long driveway. As I pulled down the driveway, I saw the two men standing in front of the house. One was in his forties and the other was in his twenties. It was obvious that they had been fighting. The older of the two, Dad, had grass in his hair and dirt stains on his shirt and pants from where they had been rolling around in the yard. His shirt was ripped and torn. Dad was also bleeding from the mouth. He had a large cut on his lower lip that looked like it was going to need stitches. I could also see what looked like a nasty cut on his right hand. His hand was by his side but I could see the blood pouring out of it.

The younger of the men, Junior, was shirtless. His jeans had grass and dirt stains on them as well. He was muscular, but not bulky. I could see Junior pointing at his dad and yelling at him as I pulled up. As I exited my police car, I could hear Junior yelling, "So you think that the police are going to protect you? We don't need the police. We can take care of this ourselves!"

The father walked up to me. Junior stood about twenty feet away glowering at us. I did not see a knife. From what I could see, his hands were clear. He continued to taunt his father, "Come on. Let's finish this right now. That cop isn't going to be able to help you."

Dad had been drinking but was not heavily intoxicated. He told me, "That's my son. He's got a bad temper, especially when he has been drinking and he has had a lot to drink."

I asked him what they were fighting about. Dad said, "I don't even know. He is in the army and is home on leave. He just graduated from Ranger School and he likes to fight. All I know is that we were in the house drinking beer and watching TV, and the next thing I know is we are out in the front yard fighting."

I asked him about the knife that Junior was supposed to have. He said, "He had a big army knife. That is how I got cut. He pulled it on me and my hand got cut when I tried to grab it. He threw it away when you got here." Dad pointed to a spot in the yard where he said Junior had thrown the knife. "Officer, I know you probably got to take him in, but he ain't going to go easy."

As if on cue, Junior came stomping over, intent on continuing the fight with his father. It was clear that he was the aggressor and I had obvious Domestic Violence charges on him. I stepped towards him and said, "Hey, sir, listen. Why don't you calm down? Why don't you give me your side of the story." I had just heard over the police radio that another officer was coming to back me up but they were still a ways off. If I could get Junior talking, I could stall for time.

Junior said, "I don't have to tell you nothing. This is none of your business."

As Junior started to step around me towards his father, I knew that the fight was on. I grabbed his right arm with the intention of using an arm bar takedown. He was very sweaty and slippery, however, and easily jerked his right arm back. Junior's hands immediately went up into a boxer's stance. He said, "OK, you want a piece of me. I'll whip you too!"

Junior stepped in and threw a right hand punch at my face. I had anticipated it and had already thrown a straight left. It connected squarely and solidly with Junior's chin. He rocked back on his heels and actually smiled at me. He said, "That was a good punch!"

That was a bit unnerving. I had hit him with a good punch and he had just shrugged it off. In reality, however, I knew that very few people actually get knocked out with one punch. It usually takes multiple strikes to stun or knock someone out so that they can be handcuffed. Before Junior could resume his attack, I pressed in and threw a series of combinations to his head and body. A few missed but most connected. The last strike that I landed was an open palm strike to the jaw. This strike caused his knees to buckle and I again grabbed his arm. This time the arm bar takedown worked and Junior hit the ground hard, knocking the breath out of him. I was able to get him handcuffed without any further problem. He had no weapons on him. I secured him in my police car. Junior was still a bit stunned and did not put up any more fight.

Sergeant Danny joined me at the scene. He apologized for the delay but said, "I knew you could take care of yourself."

I spoke to Junior's dad and got a statement from him in regards to the Domestic Violence charges. He showed me the certificate Junior had just gotten from graduating the Army Ranger training course. Dad said, "I've never seen anybody handle my son that easy."

Junior did not give me any other problems as I took him to jail. Hopefully, that arrest did not ruin his army career. I recovered Junior's knife from the front yard. It was a pretty nice Gerber fighting knife. Fortunately, Junior had the presence of mind not to bring a knife to a gun fight.

13

Crazy Dad

As domestic calls go, this one did not sound very exciting. It involved a custody dispute issue. These were almost always civil in nature and not something that we could address. The police would typically just refer the people to the Sheriff's Department since they enforce civil papers. I responded as the backup officer with Officer Shirley. The woman who called requested to meet with us down the street from where she lived. She was at a neighbor's house waiting on us.

When we got there, the woman told us that her husband had been served with divorce papers earlier in the day. She said that there was a history of physical and emotional abuse and she did not want her five year old daughter raised in that environment. She told us that her husband was mentally unstable. He was a military veteran and had seen action as a peace keeper in Lebanon. It evidently had messed with his mind because he had not held a job in several years and was addicted to prescription medicines that he got from the Veteran's Administration hospital in Atlanta. According to her, he also drank heavily.

At least, that is what the wife said. On domestic calls, there are always two sides to a story and we would have to hear his. What the wife wanted was for us to go back to the house with her and let her pick up the little girl and leave. The problem was that the divorce papers had just been served. There was no court ruling yet about who got custody of the child. We could not make him let the child leave with her mother. We could, however, check on the child's welfare and ask him to let the little girl go with her mother. That would be route that we would be attempting. If he said, "No," and the child was ok, there was not much that we could do and we told this woman as much.

Officer Chris came to the scene to see if he could assist. As it turned out, it was a good thing that he showed up. The wife showed us which house was hers and we walked over to it. Her husband, Joe, was sitting in the carport drinking a beer. He had on blue jeans but no shirt. He was a white guy and about thirty years old. We greeted him and asked him how he was doing.

He said, "Well, my wife is divorcing me so I am not doing that good."

Joe seemed soft spoken and cooperative so I thought we might be able to get this worked out without any drama. Once again, I could not have been more wrong. Joe talked, or rambled, for a few minutes about the problems that he and his wife had been having. He said that she just did not understand what he had been through and was always on his case about finding a job. He said, "It is hard to work in my condition." I asked him what condition that was. He said that he had a stress disorder. As he talked, it became clear that this was not Joe's first beer of the night. He sounded like he had had several already.

After he had talked for a while, I told him why we were there. As if on cue, little Katie came out of the house and stared at us. She had on a yellow and white sun dress. Joe saw her and called her to his side. He then looked at us and said, "Katie is staying with me. She will be fine here."

Officer Chris tried talking to Joe. He reasoned, "Don't you think that your daughter would be better off with her mother for the night?"

Joe answered, "No, I think she will be better off with me. I am not letting my wife take her away."

We all got the feeling that this was about to get nasty. The more Joe talked, the more intoxicated he was sounding. We found out later that he had also taken several pains pill to go along with his consumption of several beers. Officer Shirley, Officer Chris, and I huddled briefly. We all concurred that we could not leave five year old Katie with Joe in his intoxicated state, even if he was her father. If he had been sober, we would have already left. As it was we were not going to leave without the little girl and that was not going to be easy.

We walked back over to Joe and I told him the way that it was going to be. "Joe, you need to let Katie go with your wife for the night. You guys can work out the custody issue when this goes to court. You have been drinking a bit and we don't feel comfortable leaving her here."

Joe said, "You aren't taking my daughter and neither is my wife. You don't have any right to be here so get off my property." He was starting to raise his voice even though he was still seated.

I tried to reason with him. "Look, Joe, we don't to make this any worse, but we have to look after welfare of your child. We don't want to have to arrest you but if you force us, that is what is going to happen." What happened next was one of the most terrifying things that I have ever seen.

Without saying another word, Joe scooped Katie into his arms and stood up. He put his right hand over her throat and yelled, "You all need to get out of here. I will kill her. Do you understand? I will kill her!" I could see his fingers digging into the child's larynx.

Joe stepped towards us and yelled again, "I'm not kidding. I am going to kill her if you don't leave. My daughter is not going anywhere!"

Officer Shirley and Officer Chris were talking to Joe, telling him to stop and put Katie down. My first thought was to draw my pistol and run up and shoot Joe in the head. This was clearly a deadly force situation. Joe's fingers continued to squeeze the little girl's throat and I could see her face turning red. She weakly clutched at her daddy's hand. She only had moments left. The problem with shooting Joe was how close the child was to him. If he would choke his own daughter, he would not hesitate to use her as a shield. I did not want to take any chance of hitting Katie with a bullet intended for her dad.

Instead of my pistol, I drew my ASP baton and took a couple of steps to the left. Chris and Shirley were both still yelling at Joe and he was yelling back at them as he continued to squeeze the life out of Katie. The ASP is an expandable baton. With a flick of the wrist I had it open. The baton is an impact weapon and is designed to be used in non-deadly force situations. The typical targets that are struck with the baton are the legs and arms. In all baton training, we were always warned never to strike at the head unless it was a deadly force situation. Well, that is exactly what this was.

I was slightly behind Joe. I stepped forward and swung the metal baton as hard as I could at the base of his skull. It would probably kill him if I connected but my goal was to stop him from murdering his own daughter. He must have sensed my movement because at the moment before the baton landed, Joe ducked slightly. The blow landed heavily across the top of his shoulders. He collapsed to the ground but was still holding Katie.

Officer Chris and I dove on top of him. I grabbed the hand that was still clutched around the little girl's throat and pulled at it. He was doing everything he could to strangle his daughter. I grabbed a finger and bent it backwards until it popped. This broke his grip. Officer Shirley reached in and pulled Katie out from under us. Joe was trying to get up but Chris and I were still on top of him. We both slammed in several punches and knee strikes until we were able to jerk Joe's hands behind him and get him handcuffed. He was searched and then dragged to Shirley's police car. We weren't very gentle with him.

After he was restrained in the police car, Joe just sat there numbly. He never said a word on the way to the jail and gave no indication that he might have had a broken finger. He was charged with Attempted Murder and Resisting Arrest. We had an ambulance come and check Katie out. Physically she was fine. The emotional scars would probably take a lifetime to heal.

14

Suicide by Cop?

IT WAS ALMOST 5:00 in the morning in August of 2002. My shift was almost over. This was the toughest time of the night to stay awake. There was no traffic on the road and there were no calls pending. It was very quiet. We were hoping to coast for another hour and a half until the Day Shift came on. Instead, the radio crackled to life and dispatched us to an Aggravated Domestic call.

Who fights at 5:00 in the morning? In this case, it was a strung out crack addict who had just stumbled into the house after a night of partying. His long suffering wife had had enough and told hubby that he wasn't welcome there anymore. She wanted him out of the house and out of her life, or at least until the rent was due. Hubby did not take this news well and slapped his wife around a bit. He then pulled a pistol on her and threatened to kill her. The woman ran into the bathroom and locked the door. While hubby was trying to figure out how to break down the bathroom door in his drug induced state, the wife climbed out the window and ran to a neighbor's house.

This lady must have good neighbors because someone responded to her banging on their door and let her in and called the police for her. The first two officers arrived and met with the lady. They went back to her house and found that hubby had left again. The wife said he was driving a red Chevrolet Impala. I was in the area and I started checking the rest of the neighborhood for the car. Sure enough, he was still in the neighborhood. I saw the car sitting in the back of the subdivision in a cul-de-sac.

When I pulled up and started to get out of my police car, the Impala took off. I advised dispatch and the other officers that I was behind the vehicle in the neighborhood, heading back to the original incident location. He wasn't driving that fast; he just wasn't stopping. I had my blue lights and siren on (I'm sure the neighbors loved that!) and followed him past the house where all of this had started. He then pulled into a driveway in the middle of another cul-de-sac, a few houses down from where he lived.

I drew my pistol and crouched behind the door of the police car. His wife said that he had threatened her with a gun so I treated him as if he was still armed. I could see that the driver's window of the Impala was down so I yelled for the driver to turn the car off and throw the keys out. Surprisingly, he did what I said. I then told him to put his hands out the window. Instead, he yelled, "I got a gun. You are going to have to kill me."

I thought, *Why do people always want me to kill them? Why can't they just kill themselves and quit dragging me into it?* I said, "You don't want that. Just leave the gun in the car and get out. Keep your hands where I can see them. We can work this out."

I advised the dispatcher what was going on and requested backup. The officers at the house with the wife joined me at my pullover. I kept trying to talk with the guy, hoping he would give up. At the same time, I kept waiting for the car door to fly open and this crack head to come out shooting. He kept saying, "If you don't kill me, I'm going to kill you. I don't have anything to live for."

He wasn't going to kill us. The three of us that were there had good cover and good firing positions. If this guy came out with a gun, he was going to be very dead. Sergeant Greg arrived at the scene. By this time, there were also several other officers deployed around the car. I kept asking the guy to throw the gun out the window. I told him that we would help him. Of course, by help, I meant that if he gave up, we would not kill him and we would take him to jail. Finally, the suspect threw something out the driver's window. It looked like the magazine from a pistol. As it turned out, that is what it was. It was loaded with 9mm bullets. The suspect then said, "I got plenty more bullets. I just threw that out so you'll know I'm serious."

We already knew he was serious. He had pulled a gun on his wife. She told us that he always kept the gun with him in the car. Sergeant Greg realized what was about to happen. He also understood how this would look in the media. The newspaper headlines would read, "Black Man Gunned Down by 8 White Officers," or "Black Man Killed by White Police Firing Squad." Another consideration besides the media was the house behind the bad guy. He had pulled into someone else's driveway.

The house was less than twenty-five feet away and in our line of fire. We did not need eight officers shooting towards that house. Normally, we would have tried to get the people out, but because of how this situation had developed, that was not possible.

Sergeant Greg quickly briefed all of us, "I do not want everybody shooting if this guy comes out with a gun. Only Corporal Spell and I will engage him. Again, I do not want everybody shooting. Is that clear?"

I could see the disappointed looks on faces but I also knew that this was a good plan. Sergeant Greg and I were the two best shots at the scene. If the guy wanted to go out in a blaze of glory, we would make sure that it would be him and not us.

Both Sergeant Greg and I continued to try and talk the guy into giving up. I had thought he was smoking a cigarette, but we now realized that he was smoking crack cocaine while he tried to decide what to do. This was a bad sign. He was already acting crazy. This last bit of crack might very well push him over the edge and give him the courage to step out with his pistol.

Lieutenant Dan joined us at the scene. By now, this standoff had been going on for about an hour. Our crack head had now started telling us, "Look, I am ready to end this. I'm getting out of this car in a minute. You better kill me, 'cause if you don't I'm going to kill as many of you as I can."

Lieutenant Dan had a new toy that the firearms unit had just started issuing. They were called "Less Lethal Shotgun Rounds." They were fired through a normal pump shotgun but were designed to incapacitate rather than kill. They fired a small cloth "sock" loaded with an ounce of lead shot. They packed a punched but were not designed to kill the suspect. The Lieutenant told us he was going to move around to our left. There was tree there about twenty feet from the car. He told Sergeant Greg and me, "As soon as he starts to get out of the car, I'm going to shoot him with the less lethal. If it doesn't work, you guys take him out."

We quickly briefed the other officers. The Sergeant had already told them what to do, but we did not want anyone to start shooting when they heard the less lethal round go off. The crack head yelled out, "Ok, I'm coming out. Get ready."

Hopefully, I yelled back, "Just make sure you leave your gun in the car."

The car door opened and he stepped out. The suspect immediately turned his back to us and we could not see his hands. He appeared to be fumbling with something at his waistband, like a pistol. Why hadn't the Lieutenant shot him yet? In what seemed like several minutes, but in reality was just a few seconds, the suicidal man started to turn towards us with something in his hand. Just then the crack of the shotgun was heard. The less lethal round isn't as loud as a regular shotgun round, but there was still a loud pop. The guy screamed as the one ounce bag of lead shot crashed into his lower back, near his kidneys. He involuntarily threw his hands up over his head. I could see a shiny metallic object in his right hand. *He's still holding his pistol,* I thought. I started to squeeze the trigger of my pistol. My front sight was high on his chest, high center mass, just like they taught in the Police Academy. Before we had to shoot, however, he dropped what he was holding and collapsed in a heap on the driveway. We converged on him. Actually, the pack of officers on the scene with us converged on him. They quickly handcuffed and searched him.

While they were dealing with the crazy guy, I was looking for his weapon. As it turned out, his "gun" was a crack pipe and a cigarette lighter. He was holding them so that the crack pipe was sticking out like the barrel of a pistol. There was no gun in the car, either. The magazine that he had thrown out of the car earlier was loaded with real bullets, but the gun was nowhere to be found.

We called an ambulance to the scene to check the guy out. The less lethal round had performed flawlessly. Lieutenant Dan had hit him in a perfect spot, dropping him instantly. It left a soft ball sized welt on his lower back. The paramedics said he would be fine. He was going to be sore for a few days, but there would be no long term injuries.

The initial officer that responded to the domestic call loaded the man up and took him to jail. He was charged with Aggravated Assault towards his wife. We also found out that just before I had encountered the man, he had paid a visit to his daughter and grandson. They lived in the immediate area. He had also threatened them with his pistol, telling them that he was going to come back and kill them. This led to additional counts of Aggravated Assault.

We never did find his gun. We tore the car apart but it wasn't there. The likely scenario is that after his confrontation with his daughter, he had tossed the gun out the car window. For a crazy, suicidal person, this was pretty shrewd. If we had shot and killed him like he wanted, the media would have crucified us for shooting an unarmed man. It would not have mattered that we thought, perceived and were told by the man himself that he had a gun. Thankfully, Lieutenant Dan's less lethal shotgun round kept that from happening.

Lieutenant Dan, Sergeant Greg, and I all received commendations for our part in this incident. Major Steve wrote, "These three officers are to be highly commended for their diligence and bravery during an intense stand-off with a dangerous felon. The negotiations and use of the less-lethal option served to successfully bring the stand-off to an end and save the life of the suicidal suspect." The three of us were awarded the Departmental Officers of the Month award, my third such award.

15

Field Training Officer

DURING MUCH OF MY career before I was promoted to the rank of Sergeant, I was a Field Training Officer. Usually, Corporals are used in this capacity, but occasionally even senior Patrol Officers are utilized. I did it both as a Patrol Officer and as a Corporal. As an FTO, I would be assigned a fresh recruit to train right out of the police academy. We would ride together for three or four weeks and I would try to teach them how to apply what they had learned in the academy to the real world. Typically, a recruit will ride with three or four different FTO's before they are released to solo patrol.

Many of the recruits that I trained are still in law enforcement. I even had a few recruits get promoted to Sergeant and even one to Lieutenant before I did. That is just kind of how things worked out. That also lets you know that they were quality officers from the very beginning of their careers.

There were other recruits that you wondered how they made it through the process and got hired. I was fortunate. Every recruit that was ever assigned to me, made it through the FTO program. That doesn't mean they stuck around very long with the police department, it just means that I did my part to get them trained. Some recruits that made it to the point of solo patrol then found out police work wasn't for them. It was one thing to have an FTO with them as a safety net. Once that net was removed, however, many just could not cut it.

I trained a girl, Recruit Jennifer, who had moved down here from New Jersey to work for our police department. She had a double Bachelor's Degree in Criminal Justice and Forensic Psychology. She had a black belt in Tae Kwon Do and had competed at a national level. She did very well in the police academy and was a great recruit in the FTO program.

One night Recruit Jennifer and I responded to a serious vehicle accident. A really drunk guy had been driving really fast. He had driven off the road, over corrected, and flipped his Ford Ranger pickup truck. Now if you are drunk and going to drive like a maniac, there really is no good reason to wear a seatbelt. Our guy was not wearing his and was partially ejected as his pickup truck rolled over several times before coming to a rest upside down in a culvert. Needless to say, our drunk driver was very dead. As Jennifer was getting the information off the vehicle for her report, I noticed that she was not watching where she was standing. In my gentle and tactful way I asked her, "Do you realize that you are standing in his brains?"

When she looked down, she realized I was not kidding. His brains were smeared over several feet of the culvert. The guys head got busted open while he was hanging out and the truck was rolling over on top of him. Jennifer turned green, then pale, and came very close to vomiting. She was able to hold it in, though, and this impressed me. Most officers, especially a recruit, would have vomited.

After Jennifer completed her FTO training, however, she realized that uniformed police work was not for her. In just a few months, she was homesick for New Jersey (I guess there is no place like home, even if it is New Jersey!) and had grown tired of working accidents, mediating domestic disputes, and arresting drunks. The last I heard, she was working a nine to five job as an investigator for one of the court systems up there.

There was another recruit that had struggled to get through the police academy. His previous three FTO's had all wanted to kill him. They gave him to me as his last hope. The Major told me, "Feel free to wash him out if he doesn't improve."

I saw right away that Recruit Brian had potential. After riding with him for a few days, I felt that we could salvage him. One of the things that had alienated Brian from his previous FTO's was the fact that he wanted to argue about everything while out on a call. This is never acceptable from a recruit, especially one that has never policed before and who was riding with several seasoned and experienced police Corporals, as most of us were. By the end of our first shift together, we had an understanding. If he wanted to keep his job, he had better keep his mouth shut and do what I say. If he wanted to discuss something, we would discuss it later. And then, it had better be in a respectful tone befitting a recruit.

I realize that this might sound pretty harsh and might not fit in with a touchy feely management style. The fact of the matter is that police departments are paramilitary organizations. Structure and discipline are very important. The sooner that Recruit Brian learned this, the easier his life would be. He was already teetering on the edge of dismissal. He could not afford to alienate me like he had his other FTO's.

Another problem area for Brian was his driving. I realize that one of the reasons that people get into law enforcement (whether they admit it or not) is the fact that they get to drive fast. Brian, however, terrified me. Some calls are emergency 911 calls for help and require a fast response. Most calls, however, only require a "routine" response. We get there when we get there, and drive the speed limit. For Brian, though, every call was an emergency call. I was constantly having to tell him to slow down. This was compounded by the reality that he did not know the area that we were working in. Add these to the fact that we were working the third shift. So Brian was driving fast to every call, not knowing where he was going, in the dark. This had disaster written all over it.

As discipline, there were a few shifts in which I drove my car and made him sit in the passenger seat. For an eager recruit, this is a tough sentence. Eventually, Recruit Brian started to come around. After our three weeks together, I felt that he could do the job. I let him know, though, that if he reverted to his normal way of driving, he would lose his job. He would be too much of a liability to keep.

Within just a few weeks of solo patrol, Brian had his first at-fault car accident. A few weeks after that, he had had his second. I had transferred to a different precinct but heard that he had also been written up for Insubordination towards his Sergeant. I realized that it was just a matter of time before he would be terminated or forced to resign. The end came when he tried to drive his police car across the grass median of a divided highway. There was a piece of metal sticking up out of the ground that Brian did not see that punctured his gas tank. At the same time, his tires got stuck in the mud. This only became worse as he spun the tires deeper into the mire. When he tried to back up, he went back over the piece of metal which made a spark and set the police car's gas tank on fire. Brian was able to get out without getting hurt, but scratch one police car.

Needless to say, that was the end of Brian's short law enforcement career. Not that this is a bad thing. I'm not sure that you would want him coming to your house if you had an emergency. That is assuming that he could find you and managed to get there without getting into a wreck or burning up his police car!

Another recruit of mine, Bert, was a good one. He had played football in college on a scholarship so he was in good shape and could take care of himself. He was also smart and his people skills were good. These people skills are something that it takes some officers years to acquire. Some officers never acquire them.

What do I mean by "people skills?" Knowing how to talk to different types of people in different settings is a vital skill for police officers. The person that is a victim this week might be a suspect next week. What the public might think is that an officer who is "nice" is the one who gave them a warning ticket. On the other hand, an officer who is "mean" is the one who actually gave them an actual ticket. In reality, an officer who knows how to talk to people can give someone a ticket and have them thank him or her for it.

While Recruit Bert had pretty good people skills, he had a pretty bad sense of direction. He could not read a map and was constantly getting us lost. During our last week together before he would be released to solo patrol, we got a call to a Prowler attempting to break into a house. Since it was his last week, I was not helping Bert very much. We were about ten minutes away from the call location. After about ten minutes of going the wrong way, I finally relented and had Bert to turn the police car around. I gave him directions on how to get to the Prowler call.

We finally got there almost thirty minutes after being dispatched. We checked the outside of the house and found it secure. Bert then knocked on the door and was greeted by a very angry, older black woman. She yelled, "Where have you been? I thought somebody was trying to break into my house. I was scared. Why did it take you so long to get here?"

I watched to see how Bert would respond. This would be a good test for him. Would he get defensive? Would he get angry at the woman's emotional outburst? He said, "Ma'am, I'm sorry. I'm new and I got lost." This admission left her speechless. Bert continued, "We checked your house and everything looks fine. Would you like us to check inside?"

She said, "No, I just heard the noises outside." She thanked us for coming and we left. Recruit Bert felt bad about the situation, but this was a terrific gauge of what kind of officer he would become. It is always tough to admit you are wrong. Many officers might see this as an admission of weakness. It reality, it showed his inner strength. If we make a mistake, let's admit it and move on.

And then there was Recruit Paul. Paul was a nice kid from New York. We have hired a large number of officers from the Northeast over the last fifteen to twenty years. He had the tools to be a good officer but got homesick and eventually went back to New York, where I believe he is still in law enforcement. My only real issue with Paul was the fact that he almost killed me.

I trained him like I had trained most of my recruits, on third shift. For our department, this meant 10:30 at night to 7:30 in the morning. This is an interesting time to work. The calls that you get in the middle of the night are usually pretty interesting. If someone calls the police in the middle of the night, it is usually because they really need them. Third shift is also when we made most of our DUI arrests. This is when the drunks are trying to get home from the bars. Another aspect of third shift is the fact that this is when most commercial or business burglaries take place. One of the primary responsibilities of a third shift officer is checking businesses.

I had been working with Paul on learning how to use the ambient light so that he could turn his car lights off. The goal is to catch people committing crimes, not alert them that we are coming and scare them off. On this particular night, we were checking one of the county parks. It was about midnight and we would often find kids drinking or using drugs in one of the park's dark corners.

Recruit Paul turned the police car's headlights off as we pulled in. He drove up to the upper level parking lot. It was a dark night, but my night vision was good enough that I could see that there were no cars in the parking lot. I told Paul that the parking lot was clear and to turn around. I should have had him turn his lights on but there was another side of the park we had not checked yet. We had driven through this park several times before and I assumed Paul would have remembered that the parking lot had two levels, the upper level that we were on and the lower one.

Well, assuming things is never a good idea with anyone, but especially a bad idea with a recruit. When Paul went to turn around, he thought that the parking lot was all one level. He drove over the curb and over the six foot drop off separating the upper and lower levels of the parking lot. We had just come from getting coffee and I was holding a large Styrofoam cup of hot coffee in my left hand. Being in the passenger seat, I had the window open and my right arm outside the window. I was holding the top of the door frame with my right hand. I still had my seatbelt on. Paul had taken his off in case he needed to get out of the car quickly if we had spotted something.

As we went over the six foot drop off, into empty space, I am sure I said a lot of bad words. The police car landed on its nose and then flipped over on to its top. I was hanging upside down, thanks to my seatbelt. I felt warm liquid pouring down my head. I thought, *Oh no! I have a head wound!* Then I realized it was just my coffee that had poured all over me. My right hand was hurting but I wasn't really paying attention to it. My first problem was getting out of the upside down police car.

Recruit Paul had immediately scrambled into action. As he was scurrying out of the car, he said, "Come on, sir! We have to get out of the car!"

I said, "I would love to, you moron, but I am kind of stuck here!"

He hurried around to my side of the car and opened the door. He then helped me get unhooked, unstuck and out of the car. In his haste to get out, Paul had not bothered to turn the car engine off. It was still running and oil was evidently pouring onto the hot engine because it was beginning to smoke heavily. I told him, "Get back in there and turn the car off."

He said, "But sir, it might explode!"

That would serve him right, I thought. "I don't care," I said. "If you don't turn it off it is going to catch fire." Paul quickly crawled back in and turned the car off.

Now we had to call our Sergeant. How do you explain something like this? How do you put a police car on its top in the middle of an empty parking lot? I called Sergeant Billy over the radio and let him know we had been involved in an accident and gave him our location. I did not provide any details, I just told him we would need him to come to the scene.

The recruit was starting to panic. He said, "Corporal, I am going to lose my job for this."

I knew that they seldom fire you for one accident, even one like this. I was not about to let Paul know that, however. I figured it would probably do him good to sweat a bit. "Yep, you might lose your job for this," I agreed with him.

As we were waiting for Sergeant Billy, the adrenaline started to wear off and I realized I had a problem with my right hand. My middle finger especially was hurting and I figured that it was broken. Lieutenant Dan must have been with the Sergeant because they pulled into the park at the same time. Their expressions were priceless. The recruit's police car was totaled but it was not a very good car anyway. When I wrote my account of what had happened, I took responsibility for having Paul driving without his lights on. He was following my orders at the time and was only partially responsible for the accident. In the end, he only received a Documented Verbal Counseling Letter in regards to his driving.

Lieutenant Dan drove me to the hospital where my finger was x-rayed. The tip of the finger was crushed from where it had been trapped between the car and the pavement. The doctor said that it would heal on its own. He did not even put it in a cast. He just wrapped it and put a splint on it. Since the crushed finger was not on my shooting hand, I was back at work the next day. Needless to say, I was driving and Recruit Paul was in the passenger seat. There was no way he was going to drive my police car!

16

Foot Chase on the Interstate

RECRUIT JUSTIN AND I were on patrol one night when we saw what looked like, a stranded motorist in the median of the interstate near Buford. It was about 1:00 in the morning as we pulled up and observed a car stuck in the mud. It had been raining most of the evening and we could see where he had driven off the road into the median. Justin and I could see the tires of the car spinning. Mud and grass were spraying from behind the car as the driver attempted to get it unstuck. It was not working. The more he hit the gas, the more stuck he became.

Justin advised dispatch of our location and the tag of the vehicle and then turned his blue lights on. He parked the police car on the shoulder of the median so he would not get us stuck too. It is always good to see a recruit thinking ahead. He left a gap of about twenty feet between the two cars. As the blue lights came on, the driver's door of the car in the mud flew open and the driver jumped out and started running. It looked like a Hispanic male. The first thing that I noticed as he was running away from us was, *Those are really nice cowboy boots!*

I was not really concerned about the guy running because there was no place for him to go. The next exit was about two miles away and there were thick woods and steep embankments on both sides of the interstate. My thought was to let the man run a little ways and tire himself out and then we would chase him down in the car, jump out on him and tackle him. Nice and neat. I should have mentioned my plan to Justin. As I have said before, cops will chase anything that runs. And rookie cops really like to chase things. I saw movement out of the corner of my eye and realized that Justin was tearing off after the fleeing Mexican. The Mexican's cowboy boots were really not designed for sprinting but he was giving it everything he had. He was not able to get any traction in the grass so he started running down a lane of the interstate.

Without hesitation, Justin continued after him down the lane of traffic. Fortunately, at this time of night, there was little traffic on this stretch of interstate. It would only take one car, however, to have a tragedy. I really did not care about the fleeing drunk man (as he turned out to be). He had made his decision to run from the police. If he got run over by a tractor trailer, it would be a mess but I would not lose any sleep over it. Recruit Justin was another matter. I was responsible for him. I started yelling at him, "Let him go! Get out of the road! If you get hit, I'll get in trouble!"

By this time, the drunk had gotten about fifty yards down the road. Justin heard me yelling and slowed up. At the same time, the drunk Mexican's luck ran out and he lost his balance, falling forward on his face, landing hard on the asphalt. Justin quickly jumped on his back and handcuffed him. They were still lying in a lane of traffic. I jumped in the driver's seat of Justin's police car and drove down to where they were at and blocked the lane with the patrol car, its blue lights still flashing.

We got the winded, drunk man secured in the police car. We found out that he was very intoxicated and did not have a driver's license. He was trying to get home from wherever he had been drinking and weaved off the road, into the median, where he had gotten stuck. He was taken for a breath test to determine his level of intoxication. The intoximeter registered .28 grams, over three times the legal limit. He was charged with several offenses, including DUI, No Driver's License, and Obstruction of Law Enforcement Officers for running away from us. He had several cases of Corona beer in his car. Actually, it looked like he had consumed several cases. There were numerous empty beer bottles scattered in his back seat. There were one or two unopened cases of Corona that he had not gotten to yet.

I was very proud of how Recruit Justin had handled this call. I did counsel him about taking unnecessary risks in chasing the guy down the interstate, but his instincts were good. Our job is to catch the bad guys, not let them get away. Sometimes, we just have to vary our methods a little bit as to how we apprehend them.

17

Crazy Pregnant Lady

It was a quiet Saturday afternoon in September. It was about 5:30 and people were washing their cars, cutting their grass, or playing basketball with their kids in the Coppers Pond neighborhood. This was a nice upper middle class area. Larry lived in the neighborhood with his wife, Carmen. The only time the police ever came into that community, it seemed like, was to go to Larry and Carmen's house. We were out there a couple of times a month refereeing their domestic disputes.

Officers had learned long ago that Larry was addicted to prescription pain killers, and Carmen was just mean. The calls at their house were usually just shouting matches, but sometimes they would spill over into the front yard and the neighbors would call. On this afternoon, I received a call of a vehicle accident just up the street from Larry and Carmen's house. A neighbor had called and said that Larry had driven into his brick mailbox.

I had Recruit Lorraine riding with me. She was still in the police academy and wasn't armed. They were having the recruits come out and ride a few shifts during the middle of their academy training with the hope that it would help make sense of what they were learning in the academy. As we pulled into the neighborhood, it seemed like everyone was out doing something in their yard. When we got to the accident scene, I recognized Larry standing next to his car. He looked like he normally did, stoned out of his mind. He must have been driving way too fast when he came around the curve and lost control. He had driven up into his neighbor's yard and destroyed his nice brick mailbox. Larry's car had heavy front end damage.

Carmen was standing there with him and it looked like they were arguing. I had not been out to their house in a while and I noticed that Carmen was very pregnant, about six months along, as it turned out. As

I asked Larry what happened, I noticed that his speech was slurred and he was very unsteady on his feet. I did not smell any alcohol and asked Larry if he was still taking pain pills. He said that he was. He gave me his standard story, "I just had two teeth pulled and the dentist gave me something for the pain."

As I tried to piece together what had caused the wreck, it became clear that he and Carmen had been arguing at their house and Larry had gotten mad and left in a hurry, so much of a hurry that he wrecked into his neighbor's mailbox. At this point, Carmen started yelling at Larry and berating him for being a bad husband, a bad provider, etc. I asked Recruit Lorraine if she could try and talk to Carmen and distract her for a few minutes.

She pulled Carmen aside and asked her some questions. While she was doing this, I started to give Larry some field sobriety tests. Even though he was not drinking he was still an impaired driver. He was so impaired that when I tried to give him the first sobriety test, Larry almost fell down. At that point, I went ahead and told him he was under arrest for Driving Under the Influence of Drugs and started handcuffing him. As I was doing this I heard a loud scream from Carmen. She saw what was happening and started for me. I was still trying to get Larry handcuffed. He was not really resisting. I think he wanted to resist but he just did not have it in him that day. He was so inebriated, however, that it was taking me an extra minute to get the handcuffs on.

When Carmen started for me, Recruit Lorraine had the presence of mind to try and stop her. She grabbed Carmen's arm. Carmen was a good bit bigger than Lorraine and flung the young recruit off like she was shooing a gnat. Out of the corner of my eye I saw Lorraine land a few feet away and roll down the street. That momentary interference, however, allowed me to finish getting Larry handcuffed. I was still holding on to him as Carmen resumed her charge. She had her hands up like she was going to claw my eyes out. I did not realize pregnant women could move that fast. Just as she was about to jump on me, I raised my elbow and clipped her on the chin. I tried to make it look like I was just covering up and she had run into it. The effect was instantaneous. Her eyes rolled up in her head and she collapsed in a heap. I stuffed Larry in the backseat of the police car, and then handcuffed Carmen. By now, she had regained consciousness and was screaming at me for all she was worth. She screamed and cussed and ranted and raved at me as I put her in the car with Larry. She was already talking about suing me and the police department.

I turned to check on Lorraine. A citizen who had been watering his yard had run down to check on her. She was fine. She just had a few minor scrapes and scratches. That would give her bragging rights when she got back to the Police Academy. Then it hit me, *I am going to be on the Evening News.* The headline in tomorrow's newspaper would read, "Officer Beats Up Pregnant Woman." As I was watching my career go flashing in front of my eyes, I heard someone say, "Officer, are you ok? I saw that woman attack you."

What lovely words those were! I spoke to the gentleman and assured him that I was fine and asked if I could get a statement from him about what he had seen. As it turned out, two men had actually seen the whole incident and gave excellent written statements that supported my report. One of the gentleman stated, "I saw the screaming woman charge the officer. He put his arm up to protect himself and she ran into his elbow and fell down." Their statements also detailed how Carmen had violently flung Lorraine down the street. They also provided excellent testimony about the accident itself and said that Larry was driving at a high rate of speed and recklessly through their peaceful neighborhood.

Carmen was charged with two counts of Assaulting a Police Officer. Larry was charged with Driving Under the Influence, Suspended Driver's License and Too Fast for Conditions. It wasn't long after this incident that Larry and Carmen sold their house and moved away. The neighbors that they left behind probably threw a party to celebrate.

18

A Botched Suicide

ONE OF MY RECRUITS was a young black kid named Michael. He was only twenty two years old and was from Harlem, New York. He had never been to the South before so everything was new to him. For his first FTO assignment, he was assigned to me on the third shift at the Eastside Precinct. This area is predominantly rural, with a lot of country roads, rolling hills, and a lot of wide open space. This was a bit of culture shock for someone from Harlem. I don't know if he had even seen a tree before. I'm not sure it was the wisest thing to make his first FTO assignment at night, but those were the orders. Michael had a tough time learning the roads in the dark, but I took into account his lack of knowledge of the area and helped him learn the main roads.

On our first night together, it started off slow. The first call we were dispatched to was a burglar alarm at a business. We checked it and found everything was secure. It was probably set off inadvertently by an employee as they closed up for the night. Typically, for the first few days with a brand new recruit, I would ease them in slowly. I would drive and let them get used to talking on the radio and using the computer.

As soon as Michael advised the dispatcher that we were clear from the alarm, she directed us to start to a Person Shot call. Nothing gets the adrenaline pumping quite like those words. We were just down the road so I asked for more information. Was the perpetrator still at the scene? Do we have a description of them? What is the condition of the victim?

Dispatch came back and told us that the victim had been shot with a shotgun and it appeared to be self-inflicted. As we were pulling up to the house, dispatch told us that this was a suicide attempt but that the suspect was still alive. As I parked just up from the house, I could see two figures sitting on the ground, one holding the other, just inside the carport. As we cautiously approached, we could hear one of the subjects screaming in obvious pain. When we got close enough to see them, we could see that one of the two men was missing his face. It had been shot off. Where his face used to be was just a bloody mess. There was blood running down onto the driveway and his shirt was soaked. The other man was trying to hold a towel to the mess to stop the blood flow, but it looked like a losing battle. He was covered with the wounded man's blood.

The unwounded man was crying. He told us, "My brother tried to kill himself. Please get him some help."

I assured him that the ambulance was on its way. I looked at Recruit Michael. He was looking a little pale. Actually, he was looking a lot pale. I thought, *So, you wanted to be a police officer. Well, here you are!* This would be a good call to see what young Michael was made of.

I asked the brother where this had happened. He said there was a small outbuilding behind the house that was his brother's room. The brother said that it had happened there. I asked him if there had been anyone else present when it happened. He said that his brother had been alone at the time. We needed to go check anyway. We would need to clear the room and secure the incident scene. About this time, the ambulance pulled up. As the paramedics started treating the wounded man, getting him ready for transport, Michael and I went to check the guy's bedroom. As we walked around the side of the house, we could hear the man with no face crying out in pain as the paramedics were working on him.

Michael and I cautiously approached the outbuilding with our pistols out. You never take any chances where guns are involved. The small room was empty and we holstered our firearms. There was no question that this was where the shooting had happened. A 12 gauge shotgun lay on the bed. He must have been standing up when he shot himself because there was blood, skin, teeth, hair, etc. all over the ceiling and the far wall. There was blood on the floor and blood on the bed. All in all, it was a mess. We left the scene as we found it and went back around front try and get the whole story from the brother.

By this time, the paramedics had loaded their patient up and were headed for the hospital. The brother told us that his younger brother was very depressed. His wife had taken their two year old daughter and gone to live with her parents in Louisiana. The man had maintained hope that they would be able to patch things up. He called them every night asking them when they would be coming home. Earlier tonight, when he called to talk to his estranged wife, she told him that she would not be coming home. She was divorcing him and would be attempting to get full custody of the little girl.

The older brother had been in the house watching television when his younger brother came in and told him what his wife had said. "He was really upset," the older man said, "but I never thought he would do this."

They had talked for a while and had a few beers. The younger man then said he was going to bed. Just a few minutes later, he heard the back door slam open and his bother screaming. He found him lying just inside the kitchen with his face shot off. The older brother called 911 and attempted to care for the wound as best he could.

As best we could figure, he put the barrel of the shotgun under his chin. Angled properly, the shot would have killed him instantly. However, he either did not have the barrel positioned properly or else he flinched and moved the gun at the last instant. The shot horribly disfigured him and mangled his face. The doctor told us that the wound, while horrific, was not going to be fatal. The man's face would have to be reconstructed. It was going to be a long and painful process but he would survive. The saddest aspect of the incident is the fact that the man still has all of the same problems that he started the night with. Now he has the added problem of having no face to face them with. (Pun intended!)

Recruit Michael did a very good job on this call. He maintained his composure and did not get sick. This was an excellent learning experience for him. I could tell he was shaken up a little, but he did not let that affect him. He was able to put it behind him after we cleared the call so he would be ready for the next one.

19

An Alcoholic Pulpwooder

RECRUIT JAMES LOOKED LIKE (and still does) he should be on a Marine recruiting poster. He had actually been a recruiter before he got out of the Marines and got hired by the police department. I realized right away as his FTO that he was going to be a good officer. He learned quickly and seldom had to be told something twice.

As I was compiling material for this book, James reminded me of a domestic call that we had handled during his field training period. We got to the house in Buford at about 1:00 in the morning. Officer Bill joined us at the scene. A crying woman let us into the house and said that her husband was drunk and was threatening her and the kids. The lady's name was Mary. Her husband, Earl, was the size of two men. He was enormous! He was easily six foot five and had to weigh at least two hundred and eighty pounds. And he was very intoxicated. Mary had told us that Earl was a pulpwooder in South Georgia and only came home on the weekends. He definitely looked like he was used to picking trees up and throwing them around.

Officer Bill had been an alcoholic for over twenty years. At this point, he was heavily involved in his local Alcoholics Anonymous chapter and had been sober for over two years. He was a seasoned police officer and was great on calls like this one. He generally could talk to drunk people because he had been one for so long. I had even been with Bill on a few calls in which he had invited people to his AA meetings and they had come. Earl, however, as we would find out, was not quite ready for AA.

As you try to do on all domestic calls, we separated Earl and Mary so we could get the situation calmed down, find out what had happened, and determine if we would have to take any action. Recruit James and I talked to Mary while Bill tried to talk to Earl. James and I were just inside the kitchen and Bill was in the living room. From here I could keep an eye on Bill and we could still talk to Mary. I noticed that Earl was becoming more agitated the longer that he and Bill talked. Earl towered over Bill and I thought, *This is not going to end well. At least I have the Marines with me.*

Mary told us that she was terrified of Earl. She just knew that he was going to beat her for calling the police as soon as we left. At this point, Earl had not broken the law but we did not want to leave Mary there with him. We asked her if there was some place she could go for the night. She told us that their children were sleeping in the other part of the house and she did not want to leave them with Earl. Another option would be to get Earl to leave for the night. I could hear Bill asking him if he had any place he could go for the night. Earl's answer was something to the effect of, "I'm not leaving my house and neither is my wife. This is none of your business!"

Earl finally got tired of talking to Bill and yelled, "Mary, why did you call the police on me?"

Instead of staying in the kitchen, Mary stepped into the living room and answered, "Because you're drunk and I am tired of you yelling at me!"

Before any of us could respond, Earl crossed the living room in two strides. He moved amazingly fast for a big man and without another word, hit Mary with a backhand to the face that knocked her to the floor. I was the closest one of us to Earl. Before he could plot his next move, I stepped in and hit him on the side of the neck with the side of my hand. This technique is usually referred to as a "brachial stun." This pressure point strike, while dangerous, produces an instantaneous knockout of most people. Earl was not most people. He only staggered slightly and drew back his right hand to knock my head off. I quickly fired another, harder, brachial stun to the same place on Earl's neck. My strike landed just before his punch hit me in the face. This second shot to his neck worked. Earl collapsed in a heap to the floor. Earl's punch lost its zip and even though it hit me in the face, it did not do any damage. The three of us moved in to get him handcuffed. Because of his size, we had to use two pair of handcuffs linked together to secure Earl. Within just a few seconds, he had regained consciousness and was ready to fight some more. By this time, however, he was handcuffed and at a distinct disadvantage.

Mary had not been seriously hurt. She just had a small cut on her lip. With Earl going to jail, Mary could decide what she wanted to do without having to worry about what he was going to do to her. We never told people to get divorces or to stay together. We just tried to point them in the right direction. Officer Bill told Mary, "He is an alcoholic but doesn't want to admit that he has a problem. Until he does, and gets some help, your life and the life of your kids, is going to be like this. All you can expect is more of the same." Mary thanked Bill and told us she would be filing for a Restraining Order and a divorce the next day.

As we were putting Earl in a police car, Bill tried one more time to help him see reality. "Do you see what alcohol is doing to your life? If you don't get some help, you are going to lose everything you have," Bill told him.

When Earl told Bill to do something that is anatomically impossible, Bill just laughed at him and said to us, "That was me just a few years ago. Thank God for Alcoholics Anonymous!"

As for Recruit James, he became a very good police officer. He became part of the SWAT Team and was eventually promoted to Corporal and then to Sergeant. A few years later, I was honored to be promoted to Lieutenant on the same day that he was.

20

Vicious Dogs, Dead Dogs

IF YOU ARE AN animal lover, this chapter might disturb you. Dogs were hurt in the making of this chapter. Let me say up front that I am a dog lover. I have always had dogs as pets. At this writing, I have a pure bred German Shepherd whose parents were both working police dogs. I also have a Beagle mix that I found on the side of the road where she had been abandoned. And lastly, we have an annoying small dog of questionable heritage.

Early in my law enforcement career, I went to a house to handle a theft complaint. The complainant was not smart enough to lock his dog up before I got there and I got bit as I was ringing the doorbell. The large brown dog snuck up behind me and got me on the leg. I was fortunate that it did not break the skin. It just left a welt and a bruise. The homeowner told me that his dog was normally friendly and was surprised that it had bitten me. I educated him by giving him tickets for a Leash Law Violation and Vicious Dog. It might not normally have been vicious but it was when it bit me. This incident really impacted me. The idea of having to get a series of rabies shots in my stomach did not have any appeal to me. I decided then and there that this was not going to happen and I was not going to get bitten again.

A couple of years later, I was working Day Shift in the Lilburn area. I got a call to a burglar alarm at a home. Many of these turn out to be false, but we also get plenty of alarm calls that turn out to be actual break-ins. This alarm came in at 11:00 in the morning. This is when most people are at work and when most residential break-ins occur. Everything looked normal when I pulled up to the house. I checked the front door, all of the windows on the front of the house and the carport door leading into the house and found them secure.

Now it was time to check the rear of the house. This house had a chain link fence around the back yard. I stood at the gate and attempted to see any possible evidence that these people had a dog. If they had a dog, I would not check the back. I did not want to end up having to fight off a burglar and a dog, too. In reality, a dog in a back yard usually kept burglars out of the fence. I did not see a dog house, a dog dish, water bowl, dog toys, or anything else to indicate that these people had a dog. *They must have the fence for their kids*, I thought. Just to be sure, I rattled the gate of the chain link fence. Surely, that loud noise would alert any watch dog that an intruder was there. I waited a few moments and then opened the gate and entered the back yard.

The corner of the house was about twenty feet ahead. I did a quick peek around the corner to make sure the coast was clear. There were no bad guys with guns, but there was an eighty pound Lab/Shepherd mix coming towards me and he did not look happy. I took two steps backwards and he turned the corner of the house and charged me. He was not barking, just growling and there was no doubt in my mind he was attacking. I just managed to draw my pistol and fire one shot before he got to me. The .45 caliber bullet hit the animal behind the head on the side of the neck. He yelped and ran around behind me, falling to the ground. The problem was, now the wounded and very angry big dog was between me and the gate.

It was not a fatal shot but it had at least stopped him for the moment. I figured that there was probably a gate on the other side of the house and I started backing that way. I was not about to turn my back on the dog. I had only managed to get a few steps when I saw the big dog get to his feet, still growling and come charging again. This time I put the front sight between his eyes and squeezed the trigger. He was dead before he hit the ground.

I called my supervisor, Sergeant Eva, and told her what had happened. She came to the location. There was no one home at the house I was at, so I had our dispatcher call the alarm company who had given us the call and request that they contact the homeowner at work and have them come home. Sergeant Eva should have been the one to tell them what had happened to their dog, but she decided to go talk to the residents that lived behind the house we were at to see if they had seen what had happened.

When the man got home, I had to tell him that I had killed his dog. At first he got angry and then he started crying. When Sergeant Eva finally came back, she told the man everything that I had told her about checking to see if they had a dog before I had gone into the back yard. The man said that they had only had the alarm system for a few months and this was the first time that it had gone off. He had never thought about the fact that the police might respond to an alarm at his house and have to check the back of his residence. He said, "I should have put a sign on the fence saying that I had a dog back there." I agreed with him. That would have kept me from killing his pet.

Another time, I was driving through a neighborhood in Duluth and saw a brown Pit Bull running loose. He had the remains of a wire lead around his neck that he appeared to have chewed through. I followed him down a street to a cul-de-sac. The dog then laid down in the front yard of a house in the cul-de-sac. I had our dispatcher have one of our Animal Control Officers respond to the scene. In an effort to gauge how vicious this dog might be, I got out of the police car and stood beside it. Without hesitation, the Pit Bull charged me barking and growling. I quickly got back into the safety of the car. The dog then started circling the police car and barking. I think he was trying to figure out a way to open the doors and get to me!

A car pulled down into the cul-de-sac and pulled alongside my police car. The window came down and I could see a Hispanic lady driving. She said, "I live right there," and pointed to a house opposite of where the Pit Bull apparently lived. She continued in broken English, "That is bad dog. He attack my little dog a few months ago and my little dog have to get many stitches. I am so scared of that dog." I asked her if she had called Animal Control before and she said that she had. "They no find him because he always running loose and the people that live there are never home." I thanked her for her information.

When the Animal Control Officer arrived, the vicious dog was laying in the yard again watching us. As the officer got out of his truck, the dog jumped up and starting advancing. Animal Control Officers are not armed. They are issued a small, expandable night stick and a long pole with a noose on it for taking dogs into custody. When the police are on a scene with Animal Control, our job is to provide cover for them and not let them get hurt. I was already on the move towards the Animal Control Officer.

For some reason, however, the Pit Bull stopped at the edge of his yard. Then I saw why. A Hispanic male had come out of the house where the dog lived and had called him. This had caused the dog to stop. All the male had to do now was to retrieve his dog and secure it. We would write him several citations and that would be the end of the situation.

Unfortunately, the guy was not bright enough to figure that out. He started walking down the driveway towards us. I yelled at the man several times to grab his dog but he just kept walking in our direction. As soon as he got to the street, the dog must have seen us as a threat because he left the yard and charged the Animal Control Officer, barking and growling. I stepped in front of the officer and drew my pistol. My Smith & Wesson .45 pistol had been retired and now I was carrying a Smith & Wesson 9mm. The vicious dog was running straight towards me. At about fifteen feet I fired. The first three shots were all good hits but the angry animal kept coming. My fourth shot finally caused him to stop, turn, and run up the driveway of his house and lay down behind some bushes. All four bullets had hit him in the body.

The Animal Control Officer cautiously approached with pole and noose and tried to slip the noose around the dog's neck. Even as he was dying, the Pit Bull was trying to bite the pole. The now dead animal was secured in the Animal Control truck. The reason the dog's owner did not listen to me was because he spoke very little English. He was issued citations for Vicious Animal, Leash Law Violation, and No Rabies Tags. It is too bad that animals have to suffer for their owner's stupidity. I'm just glad I was able to deal with this vicious dog before it attacked and mauled a neighborhood child or someone else's pet.

In early 2008, I was on patrol near Lawrenceville and I heard the dispatcher give out a call for a Vicious Dog. The dispatcher said that a Pit Bull was trying to attack a subject. When I heard the address, I realized that I had just driven by there. I told the dispatcher that I would be responding as well, turned around and drove back to the house. As I pulled down the driveway, I did not see any dogs.

An older woman came to the door and told me that she had just gotten home from work. She had driven down her driveway and was about to get out of her car but a large Boxer/Pit Bull mix had jumped up on the driver's door of her car and was barking at her. The dog would not let her get out of the car. Her husband was in the house. He heard the barking and came outside with his pistol. He yelled at the dog and it ran off. He told me, "I thought about shooting it but I did not know if I would get into trouble or not."

I told him that he had probably done the right thing. When the dog ran away, it was not presenting a threat anymore. I asked them where the dog lived. They said that they thought it lived next door because they had seen it over there several times before. The house where the dog supposedly lived was several hundred feet away so I drove over rather than walk. I did not want to be caught out in the open if the vicious dog returned. I pulled down the driveway but still had to walk about seventy five feet to get to the front door. There was no sign of the dog. I did see a wire lead attached to one of the carport pillars that looked like it had been chewed through. There was also a dog dish and water bowl. This was probably the right place.

I was about halfway across the front yard when the dog showed up. I don't know where she came from but she was not happy to see me in her front yard. It looked like a Boxer/Pit mix that weighed about sixty pounds. She was definitely bigger than your average Pit Bull. She had the other end of the chewed through wire lead around her neck. Without hesitation, the angry animal charged me barking and growling. She was so fast! I drew my pistol and fired. It is embarrassing to admit, but I fired four times and missed four times. I am not used to missing but the loud noise at least caused the dog to stop briefly, and even retreat a few feet. After pausing for just a moment, however, she resumed her attack. I took my time, putting the front sight on her. My fifth shot was perfect, hitting her right behind the shoulder. She yelped, staggered backwards several steps and then collapsed on the carport next to her water dish. She was dead.

I heard the door from the house to the carport open and a young black woman stuck her head out. "What is going on?" she asked. I told her that I had had to shoot her dog. She saw the dog laying there dead in the carport and said, "That's not my dog. That's Ginger. She belongs to my roommate. That dog scares me. I have a three year old little girl and I am so scared that Ginger is going to attack her."

"You don't have to worry about that anymore," I told her. I asked where Ginger's owner was. The lady told me that he had gone to the grocery store and would be home anytime. I got my digital camera out and took several pictures of Ginger and the chewed through lead. The pictures would be attached to the report that I would write detailing the incident.

As I was finishing up, a car came pulling down the driveway. A big black male was driving and I saw a twenty pound bag of dog food sitting in the passenger seat. I thought, *I hope he kept the receipt for that.* The man got out of his car and asked what was going on. I asked him if Ginger was his dog. He said that she was. I told him what had happened. I showed him where Ginger had chewed through the wire lead. He was upset but there was not much he could say. I wrote him citations for Vicious Dog and for Leash Law Violation.

In wrapping this chapter up, I don't want the reader to think that I shoot every dog that has attacked me. I have hit several with my night-stick, flashlight, and clipboard. I have also had pretty good success in kicking them. I responded with two other officers to a domestic call in Buford. A husband and wife were arguing. When we got to their house, we discovered that these people were also not smart enough to lock their dog up before we got there.

As we entered the living room and were trying to figure out what was going on, a small dog, about ten to fifteen pounds worth, came run-ning down the hall and barking at us. He jumped up and tried to bite Officer Shirley's hand. She was able to pull her hand back to avoid being bit. The little dog then tried to bite Officer Leroy but he stepped back and yelled at the dog. It then turned towards me. The dog's owners still had not made a move to restrain him after he tried to bite the first two officers. As it charged me, I kicked it all the way across the living room. It hit the wall about three feet off the floor, bounced off, and landed hard. The little pest then got up and ran down the hall yelping.

That ended the domestic call. Whatever these people were fighting about was long forgotten. The man did not seem to particularly care but the woman was furious that I had punted her little doll across the room. They did not want to discuss their domestic issues anymore so we left. The lady called Sergeant Terry to complain but he told her to just be glad that I had not shot her dog.

21

Introduction to Car Chases

M OST OFFICERS TODAY WILL go their entire career and never get into a car chase. This is because the rules have changed. When I started my career in 1984, the only rule on car chases was to not let them get away. We would chase them until they wrecked or ran out of gas. Liability issues have changed the way that police departments view vehicle pursuits and their policies have changed accordingly.

It seems like a regular occurrence now on the news to hear of a police car chase ending in tragedy. As will be seen in the next chapter, my first car chase ended in death for the fleeing driver. In other cases, suspects have caused the deaths of innocent motorists in their attempts to outrun the police. Courts are often holding the police departments liable in civil cases in which innocent parties have been hurt or killed. The resulting financial judgments can be severe.

In an effort to protect the public, themselves, and their officers many agencies have adopted restrictive chase policies that only allow for vehicle pursuits for the most serious of crimes. My agency, for example, changed their chase policy in the mid 90s and only allows vehicle pursuits for the following crimes: Murder, Armed Robbery, Rape, Kidnapping, Aggravated Battery, and Aggravated Assault. Before the policy changed, I was in quite a few car chases. After the policy changed, I was only in one.

Our agency is very progressive in many ways. Officers are required to train in pursuit driving each year. The number of pursuits engaged in, however, is very few. It is not uncommon for a supervisor to even cancel a chase over the radio that is within policy. Even though it may be within policy, other conditions might make it too dangerous to continue. For example, a car chase at 5:00 in the afternoon is going to be much more dangerous than a car chase at 3:00 in the morning. Heavier traffic increases the likelihood that something bad will happen.

A restrictive chase policy seems to be the norm for most police departments today. That does not mean that officers enjoy watching offenders flee, knowing that they can't chase them. It requires an amazing amount of self-control to follow departmental policy and not pursue a car for a minor infraction. If the officer was able to get a tag, we can usually track them down and arrest them later. In many cases, after letting the fleeing motorist go, the officer would be waiting for them when they pulled into their driveway.

I was checking a shopping center late one night, right after our chase policy became more restrictive. It was about three in the morning and I saw a car parked suspiciously in front of a closed business. I could see that the engine was running and someone was in the driver's seat. Sure enough, as I got closer, I saw a male run out of a business and jump into the passenger seat. The business that he was running from had just been burglarized. A large rock had been thrown through the glass door. At the sight of me, they took off without having a chance to steal anything.

I activated my blue lights and sirens and went after the fleeing vehicle. I knew that Burglary was not a crime that we could chase for but I intended to pursue the vehicle just long enough to get a tag. As the fleeing suspect squealed out of the parking lot, the driver did not turn his headlights on. The car then blew through a red light, turning left and almost getting t-boned by a motorist who had the green light. At this, I immediately turned off my blue lights and siren and returned to the crime scene to do a Burglary report.

When Sergeant Rick joined me at the scene, I told him what had happened. He was an academy mate of mine and had been in a number of car chases over the years himself. He was amazed that I had let the suspect go and not pursued them. "I didn't have any choice, Sarge. That is what the new policy says," I told him.

He agreed with me, but said, "That must have been really hard letting those criminals just drive away." He was right. It was one of the hardest things I had ever done. At the same time, however, I saw this suspect come very close to causing a major traffic accident when he ran the red light. He was driving with total disregard for human life, his or anybody else's. Trying to catch him wasn't worth the risk that he would kill or injure an innocent party.

Because I was one of the first officers to be confronted by the new chase policy and to have to make a decision not to chase a fleeing criminal, Sergeant Rick wrote me a very nice letter of commendation. The Chief signed off on it and thanked me for following policy. It is always good to get letters of commendation. This was the only one I have ever gotten, though, for letting a criminal go! The next few chapters contain some of the vehicle chases that I have been involved in over the years.

22

First Chase

THE FIRST CAR CHASE that I was in was short but memorable. It was in March of 1985. The chase only lasted about two minutes but that was long enough. It was almost one in the morning on a Saturday night/ Sunday morning. I was patrolling an area near Lilburn and fell in behind a white, 1974 Pontiac Firebird. It was a nice car and built for speed. As I followed the Firebird for about a mile, it appeared that the driver might be have been drinking. The car weaved across the center line several times and then back into its lane. It then weaved onto the shoulder of the road and back.

As soon I as got to a good spot to pull the car over, I called the dispatcher and told her that I would be on a traffic stop. I gave my location, the vehicle's description, and the tag number. My police car at the time was a 1979 Chevrolet Impala. The only blue light that I had was a single light mounted on the roof. We called it a "bubble gum machine" because that is what it resembled. These old style blue lights are a real contrast to the multiple flashing blue strobe lights that police cars are equipped with today. Now, it is a light show every time an officer makes a pullover.

When the blue light came on, the Firebird just kept going. He didn't speed up right away; he just didn't pull over. We were near a big intersection and there were plenty of places for him to stop. When we got to the intersection, the vehicle turned left onto Five Forks Trickum Road and accelerated. The chase was on. I advised the dispatcher that the vehicle had not stopped and I was in pursuit. I gave her our location and turned on my siren. The Firebird was quickly pulling away from me. I saw the sports car come up quickly on another vehicle that was not going as fast. Fortunately, the driver of the other vehicle saw what was going on and swerved off the road to avoid being hit.

There is no doubt in my mind that if the Firebird had continued straight on Five Forks Trickum Road, I would never have caught him. He was already leaving my 1979 Impala behind. He could have continued for a couple of miles and turned off and I would have never found him, other than by following up on his tag information. Instead of doing that, however, the driver made a fatal mistake.

With me still in sight of him, he decided to turn onto a winding residential side street. The speed limit on Pounds Road is still just thirty five miles per hour. The Firebird accelerated to almost three times that speed. I looked down at my speedometer and saw that it was hovering around eighty five miles per hour. I knew that there was a nasty curve coming up so I backed off of the accelerator. The curve comes right after a four way stop sign. I could still see the Firebird about a quarter of a mile ahead of me. The driver never even touched his brakes as he blew through the stop sign and into the curve.

The fleeing driver had no chance of negotiating that curve at over ninety miles an hour. I saw his car slide across the center line and off the road. There is about a three foot drop off there from the road and into the front yards on that section of the street. When the Firebird left the road, it went airborne and hit a utility pole about two feet off the ground. The car's driver side door impacted the pole and snapped both the pole and the car in two pieces. Most of the Firebird's front end, including the engine block, was thrown about seventy five feet across the front yard it had landed in. When the car hit and broke that utility pole, all the power went out to the surrounding houses. A transformer attached to the pole exploded on impact and was now raining down sparks on the accident scene.

I skidded to a stop on the side of the road, alerted the dispatcher that the vehicle I was chasing had wrecked, and jumped out of my patrol car. At this time we were still carrying revolvers and I drew my four inch Smith & Wesson .357 Magnum and cautiously approached the mangled Firebird. I had no idea why the guy had run from me and I wasn't taking any chances. I could see that what was left of the sports car was tangled up in the broken power pole. Dust hung in the air. Smoke was pouring out of the wreckage. Sparks were crackling around me from the transformer. I circled around and came up to the driver's side of the car. I saw a white male hanging partially out of the driver's window. He appeared to be unconscious and was bleeding from the mouth. He was making gurgling noises as he breathed and I knew he probably was not going to make it. His legs were pinned in the car and it looked like he was going to have to be cut out of the wreckage.

I quickly checked the interior of the Firebird for passengers. There were none. Thankfully, he was by himself. At that time, we did not have walkie talkies so I had to go back to my patrol car to use the radio to request an ambulance, the Fire Department, and the local power company. I also told my supervisor, Sergeant Jim, that this was probably going to be a fatality. By the time I walked back to the wreckage, people had stopped to help and had started to come out of their houses, no doubt awakened by the siren and the crash. A man who had been driving by stopped and identified himself as a doctor. He asked me if I had checked the injured man's airway. I guess I should have, but that thought never even crossed my mind. I asked the doctor if he would mind helping me. He checked the man's airway and pronounced it clear but said that the subject had suffered severe trauma and needed immediate treatment.

The Fire Department and an ambulance arrived within minutes, but it took around twenty minutes to extract the driver from the Firebird. The paramedics did their best to stabilize him as the firefighters were working to cut him out. A helicopter ambulance was requested due to the severity of the subject's injuries. He was flown to a nearby hospital where the staff did everything they could to save him. In the end, however, the driver of the Firebird died about three hours after the chase had begun. The subject's blood alcohol level was determined to be .11 grams, which is over the legal limit.

Sgt. Jim came to the scene, where I told him what had happened. Officer Roger was one of our Fatality Accident Investigators and he came to the scene to conduct the internal investigation. Roger used the Firebird's skid marks and yaw marks to determine the vehicle left the roadway at about ninety two miles an hour. The Georgia State Patrol actually worked the accident itself. By having an outside agency conduct the investigation, it removes any hint of impropriety on our part. I was cleared of any wrong doing and Sergeant Jim summed it up when he wrote in his after action report to the Division Commander, "It is my opinion that Officer Spell conducted the chase well, and was within S.O.P. and state law during the incident."

The investigation revealed that the driver was only twenty one years old and lived just three blocks from where he died. He had just gotten his driver's license back after having it suspended for a number of traffic citations. When I tried to stop him, he knew that he was about to lose his driver's license again because he had been drinking. Instead, he lost his life.

If this incident had happened today, I am sure that I would have been required to undergo a psychiatric evaluation before returning to work. As it was, I never missed a shift. I wasn't really sure how this was going to affect me until I started having nightmares. I had recurring bad dreams about the chase and the accident for about two weeks and then I was fine. My wife, Annie, and our church were very supportive. My pastor had a pretty extensive background in counseling and he told me that the nightmares are often how our soul heals itself. Fortunately, the bad dreams ended or I might have really needed to see the psychiatrist!

23

Crashing a Wedding Reception

IT STARTED INNOCENTLY ENOUGH. The wedding reception was being held at a nice home in an upscale Lilburn neighborhood. No one ever admitted who gave eighteen year old Russell the booze that led to him getting into an argument with his girlfriend. And, of course, if you're eighteen, drunk, arguing with your girlfriend, and you have a red Camaro, the only logical thing to do is to start squealing your tires and racing it up and down the street. That is until the neighbors get tired of listening to it and call the police.

This was in September of 1990, at about 9:00 in the evening. The call came in as a Reckless Driving complaint. The dispatcher told me that the perpetrator was driving a red Camaro and was speeding through the neighborhood. Most of the time, when a call like this comes in, the vehicle is long gone before the officer gets there. We would check the neighborhood and let the dispatcher know that the suspects were gone on arrival. Tonight, however, this suspect was still there.

I saw the red Camaro in front of a house, the one with the wedding reception, as I would find out later. Russell saw me too and decided to take off. Before I had even turned on my blue lights, he was accelerating at a high rate of speed through the residential area. I advised the dispatcher that I was in pursuit of the suspect and followed him out of the subdivision. He turned his headlights off, thinking that I would not be able to see him. That did not work out so well for Russell. The chase only went about a mile up the road before Russell lost control and spun out, ending up in someone's front yard. The Camaro took out a really nice flower bed. It's tough to drive at night if you are drunk and can't see where you are going.

As I pulled up, however, the Camaro drove out of the flower bed, out of the yard and back down the road in the direction that we had just come from. This time, Russell drove back into the nice neighborhood where this had all started and back to the wedding reception. He jumped out of his car and ran into the house. By now, I had another officer with me, Officer Molly. She and I chased Russell into the house and tackled him in the large living room. As we were handcuffing him, I noticed that there were probably sixty people standing there watching us and they all had on nice evening gowns or tuxedos. We were on the floor next to a large table with a beautiful punch bowl on it.

After I got Russell handcuffed, the owner of the house, wearing an expensive tuxedo, came stomping up demanding to know what was going on. I told him that the young man that I had just arrested was squealing his tires and driving recklessly in the neighborhood and several of his neighbors had called the police to complain about it. This shut him up for a minute, but it was clear that he was embarrassed at this unscheduled entertainment. It became quickly apparent that Russell was also drunk and I let the homeowner know that he might be responsible for that as well.

As Molly and I were escorting Russell out of the house, another of the guests demanded that we let them handle the situation. I just laughed at him and kept going. A couple of the other men in tuxedos started talking about whether or not we had any right to be there. We got Russell secured in my police car. I was unable to determine whether or not his Camaro had any insurance, so I called for a wrecker to impound it. This required us to stay in front of the house with our blue lights activated for about another twenty minutes waiting for the wrecker to arrive. This was very embarrassing for the homeowner. He asked me several times if we could just take Russell on to jail and leave his car there. "Not a chance," I told him. And to stir the pot just a little more, I added, "You might want to apologize to your neighbors for Russell's little escapade."

When the wrecker got there, the homeowner summoned the rest of his dignity and told Molly and I that he was going to file a formal complaint on us for crashing his party. We laughed at him and I said, "You do that. My suggestion is that next time you might want to be a little more discriminating about whom you invite to your party and who you serve alcohol to."

Russell was charged with DUI, Fleeing and Attempting to Elude Police, Reckless Driving, Driving without Headlights, and Driving on the Wrong Side of the Road, and No Insurance. I never had to go to court on him. He evidently worked out a plea deal, lost his driver's license for a year or so and paid his fines.

The homeowner never did file a complaint, but his attitude left me with a bad taste in my mouth. I called a friend of mine that worked for the local newspaper. I told him that I had a story that needed to get into the local section. He owed me a favor and was more than willing to comply. The heading was "Man Arrested at Wedding Party." It was nine paragraphs long and almost reproduced my entire arrest report. It included Russell's name, his charges, and the address where the incident took place. I figured the neighbors might want to know what was going on in their plush neighborhood.

24

The Sports Shoe Bandit

IN EARLY 1991, OFFICER Charlie was sitting in the darkened corner of the shopping center in his police car watching the Sports Shoe store through his binoculars. This store had been broken into three times in the last month. It sat less than a mile from the Dekalb County line, on Highway 78, near Stone Mountain, making it an easy target. The perps usually hit between 3:00 and 5:00 in the morning. They would throw a brick through the glass front door and each time, they had made off with thousands of dollars of shoes, clothes, and accessories. A brick through the door activated the burglar alarm system, but the perps were long gone by the time an officer showed up to check the alarm.

We had been trying to keep an eye on the business as best we could. The burglars were overdue and we all felt that it was just a matter of time before they would strike again. Officer Charlie had been watching the store for about an hour. There were several of us that were in the area waiting for Charlie's call. We all had Citizen's Band radios installed in our police cars so that we could talk informally without tying up the police radio.

The CB crackled to life around 4:00 in the morning. Charlie said a car had just pulled up to the Sports Shoe with its lights out. He narrated what he was seeing as the rest of us quickly moved that way. A black male had gotten out of the car, carrying a big rock. Without hesitation, he threw the rock through the glass front door and ran into the business. Moments later, he ran out carrying armloads of expensive starter jackets, jogging suits, and other designer sports clothes.

Four marked police cars came screaming across the empty parking lot of the shopping center. As we converged, the burglar was just coming out of the store with his second load of clothing. He saw us coming and jumped into the driver's seat of his green Trans Am. I was approaching head on to the Trans Am. Our goal was to block the subject in and to make a quick arrest. It did not work out like we had hoped. I pulled up on the driver's side of the perp's car. Another officer was to my left, effectively blocking the guy in. Or so we thought. Other officers were coming from the rear and were parking behind him. My headlights were shining into the passenger compartment. We jumped out of our cars with our pistols drawn and yelled for the suspect to get out of his vehicle with his hands up.

I could see that the suspect's eyes were glazed over. He looked around at all of us and then aimed his Trans Am straight at me. He accelerated quickly. I dove back into the police car just as the Trans Am hit my left front fender and driver's door. He continued to accelerate after hitting my car, actually pushing the police Ford Crown Victoria out of the way. As soon as he had his opening, the burglar blew through the hole and was racing across the parking lot.

The Ford Crown Victoria is a tough car. Even though it had taken a significant hit from the Trans Am, I was still able to drive it. I was not about to miss this chase. It was personal now. The fleeing burglar was almost to the other side of the parking lot. From the exit he was approaching, he could go two ways. He could turn right, which would put him back out on Highway 78. All he would have to do then was to make a quick left turn and he would have a good chance of escaping. The county line was less than a mile away. We would chase him into Dekalb County, but he had a significant head start and a good car to flee in.

The other option leaving the shopping center was to turn left. This would put him on Bermuda Road, a narrow, weaving road that went around Stone Mountain. Now, the road has been changed. When the Atlanta Olympics were held in 1996, Olympic tennis was held at Stone Mountain Park. A large tennis stadium was built on Bermuda Road. This stadium was not there in 1991. If our bad guy turned left, it would not be as easy for him to get away.

The other three officers anticipated that the perp was going to get on the highway and head for Dekalb County. It was a good guess. It just was not the right one. You can't predict what a scared crack head will do. I was a little slower getting back into the chase after getting banged pretty hard. The other three officers took a short cut out of the shopping center and got on Highway 78, hoping to catch up with the Trans Am before it got too far ahead.

I followed the tail lights of the burglar's vehicle and saw him turn left instead of right out of the shopping center. *Bad move for you*, I thought. The speed of the Trans Am was nullified on Bermuda Road's curves. I notified the other officers of our direction of travel. I knew it would be several minutes before they joined me, however. They would have to go down to the next exit and turn around and come back. It was clear that the burglar did not know where he was. He almost lost it in the first two curves we went through. As fast as he was going, I knew it was just a matter of time before he wrecked.

The next curve did the trick. The perp lost control and left the road, smashing into a ditch and then a fence running around the outside of Stone Mountain Park. I could see that three of the Trans Am's tires had been flattened on impact. I jumped out of the police car with my pistol drawn. The S&W .45 was held in a low ready as I yelled at the suspect to put his hands up. I could see that the driver's window was down. The black male started to put his hands up and then I saw his right arm go down, as if he was grabbing for something under the seat. The front sight of the .45 found the bad guy's head and I started to squeeze the trigger. I told him again to put his hands up. The perp looked down the big barrel of my pistol and quickly complied.

Looking back, I know that I should have waited on backup officers to get there. The truth was I was still pretty hot about this guy trying to run over me. I also did not want to give him an opportunity to try and get out and run on foot. My adrenaline was pumping. I stepped up to the Trans Am, quickly holstered my pistol, and then snatched the burglar through the driver's window. I threw him to the ground. The bad guy made the mistake of trying to get up. A few quick punches to his back and head stunned him long enough for me to get him handcuffed. Sergeant Gerald pulled up and helped me get the bad guy secured in my patrol car.

Officer Charlie went back to the Sports Shoe to meet with a manager so that he could make a Burglary report. He eventually took custody of the prisoner and transported him to the jail. As it turned out, the Trans Am had been stolen from the other side of Atlanta. The ignition had been popped. The burglar had also disabled the interior light of the car so that it would not come on when he opened the door. It was obvious that he had done this kind of thing before. He was charged with Burglary, Aggravated Assault on a Police Officer (me), Motor Vehicle Theft, and

Possession of Cocaine, as well as numerous traffic charges related to the car chase. He had had the two ounces of cocaine hidden on himself and had tried to dump it in the back of Charlie's police car.

The detectives ended up charging this guy with multiple counts of Burglary after interviewing him and executing a search warrant at his residence. He was making a pretty good living selling the stolen clothes in Atlanta or trading them for drugs. He ended up working out a plea deal when his case came up for trial. He was sentenced to a pretty lengthy prison term for his transgressions.

25

Drunk on a Motorcycle

I WAS WORKING ANOTHER third shift in Buford. It was August of 1995 and the dispatcher sent me to look for an intoxicated man pushing a motorcycle in the roadway and creating a traffic hazard. It was almost 11:00 at night. When I got to the area, I quickly saw why someone had called the police. I saw a man sitting on a motorcycle, trying to roll it down the road. It would roll a ways and then he would put his feet down and run, kind of like Fred Flintstone, to get some speed up, and then repeat the process. He did not have the light on his motorcycle on and traffic had started to backup behind him.

When I turned my blue lights on to stop the motorcycle, the driver turned and looked at me. Instead of stopping, he put his feet down and ran a little ways to propel the motorcycle along. The engine of the motor-cycle wasn't on and this guy was trying to outrun me! He repeated this process for almost one hundred yards. Realizing he could not get away, the driver finally pulled over onto the shoulder.

I asked the driver to get off the motorcycle. He was huffing and puffing from his exertion. When I asked him for his driver's license he said, "I wasn't driving." He gave me an ID card. I could smell the alcohol on the guy from five feet away. He could barely stand and had to lean against his motorcycle. I don't know how he had kept it upright while he was riding it.

I asked the man where he was coming from. He said, "Right here," slurring his words. We were standing on the side of a four lane highway. There were no houses around so I thought he might have misunderstood me. I asked him again where he was coming from. This time, he pointed down and said, "Right here." I had already asked the dispatcher to check the registration information on the motorcycle's tag. When I asked the driver if he had insurance on his motorcycle, he said, "It's not my motorcycle." The dispatcher came over the air and told me that the motorcycle was registered to a Steve W. I looked at the ID card the guy had given me and saw the name "Steve W." I said, "The bike is registered to you." He said, "Well, yeah, it is my motorcycle."

It was clear that Steve was heavily intoxicated. I asked him how much he had had to drink. He said, "I'm not driving." Since this conversation was obviously getting me nowhere, I went ahead and arrested him for Driving Under the Influence. When I checked his driver's license, I found that it was suspended and he was a Habitual Offender. As soon as he was handcuffed and in the police car, Steve started cursing and yelling at me. He said, "You people must be hard up for money to arrest a man for pushing his motorcycle."

The engine of the bike was still warm. In between the drunk's tirades, I learned that he had run out of gas about a mile up the road. There was a gas station at that location but it had already closed for the night. Rather than leave his bike there, Steve decided to try and get it home. He was still about a mile from his house when I found him creating the traffic hazard.

When it came time for this case to go to court, Steve hired a lawyer who tried to argue that he was not really "Driving" under the influence because the engine of the motorcycle was not on. He was only rolling the bike. The lawyer asked me several times if the engine of the motorcycle was on when I had stopped his client. He was trying to drive his point home. Each time, I would answer the lawyer very politely, "No sir, the engine was off when I encountered your client riding his motorcycle down the middle of the road, at night, with its light off. The engine was warm, indicating to me that the engine had been on recently but it wasn't on when I encountered him creating the traffic hazard that led to his arrest."

I answered several of the lawyer's questions with this answer so I could make sure that the jury understood what I had seen on the night that I arrested Steve. In the end, the jury convicted Steve of DUI and a number of other traffic offenses. Because of his extensive history of DUI arrests and other traffic offenses, he was sentenced to two months in jail and some expensive fines.

26

Car Chase and Fight with a Lady of the Night

FOR A SMALL TOWN, Buford has always had more than its fair share of criminals. The drug activity there is legendary. In the late 80s and through the 90s, people were driving from all over North Georgia to buy their illegal drugs. You could get crack cocaine, powder cocaine, marijuana, and methamphetamine pretty easily. If you wanted something besides drugs, prostitutes were also available. On most nights, these ladies could be seen out walking the streets trying to pick up a "date." They were a sad lot because every one that I ever talked to was hooking to support their drug habit. I don't know of a single one that I ever dealt with that was not a crack addict.

I was patrolling an area of the city one night that was known for its crack houses. This was the section of town that was predominantly African-American. A white person always stood out in this community, especially in the middle of the night. If you stopped a white person driving through this area, they had just bought drugs or were about to. It may sound like I am stereotyping but that is just the way that it was.

I saw the white girl standing next to a car that was parked in front of a mobile home that was well known as a crack house. She was short, stocky, and was wearing shorts and a pink tube top, the basic prostitute uniform. The guy who lived in the mobile home had the street name of "Peanut." I never found out what his real name was. Peanut had been in and out of prison for years for selling drugs. Because he wasn't a violent criminal, he would only serve a few months and then be released. Once he was out, Peanut would start selling again. When the white girl saw me, she got in the car, a black Ford Escort, and took off.

She blew through the stop sign just up from Peanuts trailer, so I turned on my blue lights and tried to stop her. She accelerated and the chase was on. I activated my siren to go with the blue lights and tried to

avoid hitting the many cars that were parked in the street in this residential neighborhood. I advised the dispatcher that I was in a chase and
gave my location. As fate would have it, all the other zone cars in my area
were tied up on serious calls themselves and I was on my own, at least for
a little while. The Escort sped up and down several of these residential
streets. It was amazing that she did not wreck. The chase only lasted for
a few minutes and she started to work her way back towards Peanut's
trailer. Sure enough, she drove back to the trailer and stopped, jumped
out of the Escort, and tried to run.

She only had on flip flops so she could not get much traction. I
caught up to her after a short foot chase and grabbed her by the arm. At
that, the fight was on. She started punching and kicking and screaming
at me. Every blow that she threw missed, but I needed to get her to the
ground so I could control her. I kicked her feet out from under her and
dropped her on her face. She continued to fight, throwing elbows at me
and trying to buck me off. She was still screaming and I noticed that
people had started to come out of their homes to see what was going on.
Nobody tried to interfere. I think if it had been a black girl or guy, some
of the bystanders might have become involved. As it was, everyone just
watched the show.

After a few minutes, I was able to get one handcuff on, but her other
arm was under her and I couldn't get to it because of how violently she
was struggling. She was surprisingly strong. Then I had an idea. I had
never used my pepper spray on anyone before. Why not now? If this
had been a guy, I would have just pounded him into submission. I really
could not do that with a girl. I grabbed the pepper spray off of my belt
and held it about an inch from her face and gave her a good long burst.
She screamed even louder now. I told her to give me her other hand. She
told me to do something that was physically impossible so I sprayed the
rest of the can into her nose and eyes.

Pepper spray produces a physiological reaction. When sprayed with
the cayenne pepper mixture, it causes the eyes to close and constricts the
breathing passages. It is hard to fight if you can't see or breathe. It is
also extremely painful. Before they let us carry pepper spray, we all have
to get sprayed with it so that we know what it is like. It is painful and
uncomfortable but it is not the end of the world. You can train to fight
through it so that if you are ever sprayed yourself, you can handle it.

When I gave this girl the rest of my can of pepper spray, she had had enough. She quickly put her other hand behind her back so I could handcuff her. After I had her under control, my backup units finally started arriving. As per our policy, after I had the girl under control, I tried to pour some water into her eyes and wash out the pepper spray. The problem is that while water makes it feel a little better, it takes several hours before it stops burning. So, as I was driving her to the jail, she screamed and cried and begged me to pour some more water in her eyes.

She was charged with several serious traffic charges, as well as Possession of Cocaine. I found the crack rock in her car. She had just bought it and had not had a chance to smoke it yet. She was on probation for a previous drug arrest and also had an active warrant for Failure to Appear from the last time she had been arrested.

After knocking on Peanut's door for several minutes, he finally opened it. He probably had flushed all his drugs down the toilet. I asked him about the girl. He said, "Mr. Spell, I don't sell drugs anymore. I'm clean. I just got out and I'm working at the Waffle House. I have a career now. I don't know who that girl is." Somehow, I wasn't convinced.

27

Long Chase with an SUV

I HEARD THE YOUNG officer go out on a traffic stop on Buford Highway, inside the city limits of the city of Buford. I was nearby so I went to check on him. This was in January of 2001, at about 12:30 at night. When I pulled up, I saw that he had a gold Chevrolet Tahoe pulled over. I could easily see why he had stopped him. Instead of a tag, there was a piece of cardboard displayed that said, "Tag Applied For."

Officer Chris told me that the driver did not have a driver's license with him and the name he had provided had not come back on the computer. When this happens, it almost always means that the person has given us a false name. Of course, if the person is unlicensed there will not be a return, but most Americans have a driver's license if they are eligible for one. The usual reasons that people lie about their name is because they know that there are warrants out for their arrest or that their driver's license is suspended or revoked. An easy way to verify someone's name is to get them out of the car and check to see if they have a wallet. A lot of time the people who have told you they don't have their driver's license with them, have just "forgotten" that it was really in their pocket all along. In Georgia, it is a misdemeanor to lie to the police about your identity. It is also a misdemeanor not to produce your driver's license when the police request it.

Chris went back up to the Tahoe and spoke to the driver again. We asked who the vehicle belonged to. He told us that it was his father's vehicle. A computer check of the Tahoe's vehicle identification number showed that it should have a tag displayed on it. It came back to a man with a different last name than what the driver had given us. Things were not really adding up. The young man that we were dealing with told us he was eighteen years old, so we should have been able to get something when we ran him on the computer.

Chris attempted to call the owner of the vehicle. Our driver, Timothy, had given us his father's phone number. At least, that is what he told us. When Chris called the number, he got the voice mail for what sounded like a young male named "Christopher." In fact, Chris said, the voice sounded a lot like Timothy. We both began to feel that the Tahoe was probably going to be stolen. Officer Chris decided it was time to get Timothy out of the Tahoe and secured in a police car until we could get things sorted out.

When we walked back up to talk to Timothy, however, he refused to open the car door. We asked him to step out. He asked, "Am I going to jail?"

Chris told him, "No, but we have to verify who you are and who owns this vehicle."

Timothy then put the Tahoe's window most of the way up and said, "I'm not getting out of the car. I know y'all are going to take me to jail."

Chris told him that if he did not exit the vehicle immediately, he would definitely be going to jail. At this, Timothy put the window all the way up. I grabbed the driver's door handle but found that the doors were locked. Timothy then put the Tahoe in drive, jerked the steering wheel to the left and floored the accelerator. Chris and I both had to jump out of the way. We had to jump into a lane of Buford Highway to avoid getting run over. Fortunately there was no traffic coming.

Officer Chris and I both jumped into our police cars and took off after the Tahoe. At that time of night, there was minimal traffic on the road. As the more experienced officer I took the lead in the chase. The county line was only about three miles North of where we were so I asked dispatch to notify the next jurisdiction, the Hall County Sheriff's Department, that we were headed into their county.

We only got up to about eighty miles an hour, but the Tahoe was driving erratically. He passed several cars on a double yellow line and forced other vehicles off the road. At one point, he was completely in the oncoming lane, playing "chicken" with oncoming traffic. Clearly, if we did not get him stopped, someone was going to get hurt. Within just a couple of minutes, we left Gwinnett County and were in Hall County. Chris and I were still the only two officers involved in the chase.

Our dispatcher advised that the Hall County deputies were going to deploy "stop sticks." These are designed to puncture the tires of a fleeing vehicle, forcing them to stop. The first time they deployed them, the

Tahoe managed to get around them. A Hispanic family, in their older model Nissan Maxima, were not so fortunate, however. They drove over the stop sticks and punctured all four of their tires. While they were definitely inconvenienced, they did get a new set of tires out of the deal, courtesy of the Hall County Government.

The second time that the stop sticks were deployed, a little further up the road, was the charm. The Tahoe drove over them and punctured both his front tires and his right rear one. Timothy did not stop right away, however. In fact, he kept going for several more miles. The punctured tires did keep his speed down. After a couple of miles, his punctured tires started coming apart and slamming into the side of the Tahoe. Within another mile or so, he was driving on three rims. The sparks were flying as the suspect continued to try and get away.

By now, we had a number other police cars from three different jurisdictions, Gwinnett County, Hall County, and the City of Gainesville involved in pursuing the suspect. The car chase had lasted almost seventeen miles and gone on for fifteen minutes. The perp made one last ditch effort to get away by turning down a side street just as we came into Gainesville. The Tahoe was difficult to control with three of its tires gone. Timothy spun out in the middle of the road. Police cars swarmed around and blocked the Tahoe in. Hall County deputies and City of Gainesville officers rushed up to the vehicle and drug young Timothy out. They slammed him down hard on the pavement. Timothy made the mistake of trying to get up and got smacked around a bit for his trouble. The deputies quickly got him under control and held him so that Chris could handcuff him. Timothy ended up with a few minor scrapes and scratches on his face.

Now that he was under arrest, the young man started talking. He said that his name was really Christopher. He was fifteen years old and did not have a driver's license. The truck really did belong to his dad. He had snuck out of the house, "borrowed" the truck, and was going to visit his girlfriend. He really could not give us a good reason as to why he had removed the tag. It had probably seemed like a good idea at the time. He apologized for lying to us but said he was scared.

If he had been honest with us at the beginning, he would have gotten a ticket for Driving Without a Driver's License, and we would have called his father to come and get him. That might have been a bit painful and embarrassing, but it would not have been nearly as bad as it ended up. Christopher ended up getting multiple traffic citations, including No Driver's License, Reckless Driving, and Fleeing or Attempting to Elude the Police. He was arrested and placed in the Youth Detention Center until his hearing the next day. These tickets would prevent Christopher from getting a driver's license for several years and there would also be substantial fines involved.

On top of all that, Christopher had trashed his dad's Tahoe. It was going to need three new tires and rims. It had substantial body damage where the tires slammed into the fenders as they were coming apart. The vehicle had been impounded and his father was going to have to pay to get it out of impound. This was a real learning experience for young Christopher. Fortunately, no one was hurt. At least he had a great story to tell the girl about why he did not show up for their romantic meeting!

28

Meeting a Legend

IN 1996, I GOT a phone call from a close friend. Officer Hal and I had worked together on and off for years. He was currently assigned to the Motors Squad. These are the officers that ride those big police motorcycles. Their primary responsibility was traffic enforcement. They ran radar all day and issued citations in various areas in an effort to reduce traffic accidents. No one that I know of has ever accused our agency of running a speed trap. There is so much traffic in Gwinnett County and so many people speeding, officers seldom write a speeding ticket for any less than fifteen miles over the speed limit.

Motor officers did have a number of other responsibilities. One of the biggest was that of providing motorcycle escorts for VIPs, funerals, and the occasional parade. On the day that I got the phone call, I was off. Hal greeted me with his standard, "Hey, boy! What are you doing?"

I told him that I was off and did not have much going on. He said, "Put your uniform on and drive down to Richard's Middle School. I have somebody I want you to meet."

For me to get dressed in uniform and to go somewhere on an off day would generally mean that I would be working a part time job and getting paid very well. I asked Hal who it was that he wanted me to meet.

Hal said, "Hey, if you're too busy, that's ok. I'll just tell him that you couldn't make it."

My curiosity was really aroused. "You have to tell me who it is, Hal," I told him. "You know I'm not going to drive across the county if I don't know what you are talking about." In reality, I would only have to drive about four miles, but that was beside the point.

Hal hooked me. "Do you want to meet Muhammad Ali?" he asked.

I didn't ask for any more details. I just said, "I'll be right there," and hung up. I put on my uniform, jumped in my police car and was at the school within twenty minutes of Hal's call. I have been a boxing fan all my life. I was about thirteen years old when I first saw the "Thrilla in Manila" replayed on network television. This heavyweight title fight between Muhammad Ali and Joe Frazier was one of the greatest boxing matches in history. When I saw this fight, I became not only a boxing fan, but also a Muhammad Ali fan. The "Thrilla in Manila" was the last great fight that Ali had. He only fought for a few more years so I became a fan late. All of his fights have been replayed on television and you can watch them today on the internet or buy them on DVD.

To have a chance to meet Ali was an honor that I was not about to miss. I actually had a few of my Christian friends criticize me later because I mentioned that I had met Ali. "He is a radical Black Muslim. Why would you want to meet someone like that?" I was asked.

My answer was not very profound. "He is also one of, if not the greatest boxers ever. He is one of the most gifted athletes in history. Maybe I should, but I really don't care about his religious beliefs. Like all of us, Ali will have to answer to God one day. I am not his judge."

When I pulled my police car into the parking lot of the Richard's Middle School, I saw that Motors Unit had their motorcycles parked in a line and the officers were standing beside their bikes as if they were waiting on something. I parked and found Officer Hal. "Hey buddy!" he said. "He will be here in just a little while. Just act like you are with us."

While we were waiting, Hal filled me in. Ali was in Atlanta with author Thomas Hauser. Hauser and Ali had just released a book that they had co-authored about Ali's life. They were making appearances and promoting the book. I was a little puzzled about why they were at a middle school. Hal said that the only two stops in Atlanta that they were making were at an intercity school in Atlanta proper and a stop at a suburban middle school, Richard's in Gwinnett County.

Hauser is a prolific writer, mostly in the area of sports. He has actually written several about Ali and a number of others about boxing in general. One of the best books that I ever read about boxing was Hauser's, *Black Lights: Inside the World of Professional Boxing*.

After waiting for just a few minutes, a large charter bus pulled up. I recognized Thomas Hauser as he got off. The next person off the bus was Pete Van Wieren. Van Wieren is a well known personality in Atlanta.

For thirty two years, he was one of the voices of the Atlanta Braves. He provided commentary on radio and television. Hauser and Van Wieren both stood in front of the bus and waited for everyone else to exit it.

The Motors Unit was at the school as an honor guard for Ali. When the meeting at the school was finished, the Motors Unit would then escort the bus on their way out of town. When Ali stepped off the bus, he immediately walked over to the line of police officers standing beside their motorcycles. Ali walked slowly and deliberately, a result of the Parkinson's Disease that was wracking his body. He started at the end of the line of officers and worked his way down it, shaking hands with each officer.

I was on the far end of the line standing next to Hal. When Ali got to me and shook my hand, I said, "Nice to meet you, Champ."

Ali stopped, still holding my hand, and leaned towards me. He talks in a raspy whisper, again the result of the Parkinson's Disease. As he leaned towards me, he whispered, "What did you call me?"

I said, "I called you 'Champ.'"

At that Ali's eyes twinkled and he let go of my hand. He said, "Ah, I thought you called me a 'chump.'"

School officials then escorted the entourage into the school. There was going to be a school assembly in Ali's honor. He was ushered into a room backstage until it was time to start. They wanted two officers to stay with Ali at all times. Somehow, Hal and I got chosen for this honor. While we were waiting, we took the opportunity to get our picture made with the Champ. I wonder how many thousands of times Ali has had his picture taken with complete strangers. I still have that photo on my desk.

Ali's wife was part of the entourage. We found out that she actually speaks for him at these events. It was interesting to watch Ali and his wife as we were backstage. She and the school officials chatted. I was talking to Hal when I heard something buzzing in my ear. It sounded like a mosquito. I turned to swat at it and saw that the Champ was standing behind me. He could rub his fingers together so that they made a buzzing sound. When he saw that he had "gotten" me, his eyes twinkled again and he smiled. It is a shame that I never got to meet him when he was in his prime. There is no doubt that he would have been the life of any party.

When the time came for the assembly, Ali was led into the auditorium. Hal and I stayed close to the front, near the stage. There were several hundred middle schoolers in the assembly but they were all very well behaved. The assembly consisted of Pete Van Wieren speaking for a few minutes and then introducing Thomas Hauser. Hauser then discussed the book that he and Ali had co-authored. I believe the title was, *Muhammad Ali in Perspective.*

After Hauser finished, he introduced Ali and his wife. She walked over to the podium and Ali stayed seated on the stage. She talked for a couple of minutes about Ali's life and the challenges that he faced with Parkinson's Disease. She opened the meeting for questions. They had a microphone set up down front. The only question that I remember was one from a young man who asked Ali, "What was your toughest fight?"

Ali's wife leaned over him and he whispered his answer in her ear. She laughed and straightened up. She addressed the student, "He says that his first wife gave him his toughest fight."

When the meeting ended, we escorted the Champ out of the assembly hall and back to the bus. I am still not quite sure why they chose to have Muhammad Ali appear at a middle school. I doubt any of those kids had ever even seen replays of Ali's fights or had any idea what a great fighter and personality he had been. At the same time, I was thrilled and honored to have had the opportunity to meet the Champ.

29

One Dangerous Guy

ONE OF THE BEST assignments that I had during my career was as a Sergeant in the Crime Suppression Unit. Crime Suppression was assigned to Tactical Operations and focused on Violent Crimes, such as Armed Robbery, as well as gangs and drugs. We also assisted the Narcotics Unit and other Detectives in serving high risk warrants. Tactical Operations is the police version of the military's Special Forces. Each of the units assigned to Tac Ops has a specific mission. The officers are highly trained, highly motivated and represent some of the best officers in the Department.

Crime Suppression is essentially a tactical unit. Most of the officers in the unit are also on the SWAT Team. The entire unit, SWAT or not, received extra training in room clearing tactics, vehicle assault tactics, drug enforcement, and gang recognition. While most of Crime Suppression's work is done in uniform, we also had several undercover cars assigned to us. These were not just unmarked police cars. They ranged from a minivan, to a pickup truck, to a couple of passenger cars. These vehicles allowed us to conduct surveillance without alerting our targets that they were about to have a bad day. We all packed a set of plain clothes with us just in case a situation arose that would require an undercover approach.

A couple of times a week, I would get a call from a Sergeant in the Narcotics Unit or from the Violent Crimes section in our Detective Division asking us to help them serve warrants or to help them locate someone. I had just walked into my office one evening when I got such a call. Sgt. Will was a Detective Sergeant in the Violent Crimes Unit. His detectives investigated Murder, Armed Robbery, and other violent crimes.

Sgt. Will told me that a judge had just signed a Murder warrant on a subject and they needed him located and arrested. Will said that the suspect belonged to the violent Hispanic street gang, MS13. This gang origi-nated in Los Angeles among immigrants from El Salvador. They have a reputation as being one of the most violent gangs in the United States. While they have traditionally been a West Coast gang, their presence in the Southeast is increasing every year. Their violence often targets rival gang members. In this case, three MS13 members shot and killed a rival Brown Side Locos member a couple of months earlier. BSL is another violent Hispanic gang that has a strong presence in and around Atlanta. We were coming into contact with more and more MS13 members and knew that they were usually armed and not afraid of the police.

Will and his detectives had already arrested two of the MS13 gang members that had killed the "victim." As most criminals do, when they were interviewed, they quickly gave up the third member of their hit team, Juan. They told the detectives, though, "You will never take Juan alive. He has said he will never go back to jail. Either he will kill the police or they will kill him." The two arrested gang members also freely admitted their own fear of Juan and talked about what a bad dude he was.

When Sergeant Will called me, he gave me all the information that he had. He told me about Juan's statements that he would not be taken alive. His criminal history showed arrests for Armed Robbery, Aggravated Assault, and drug charges. The only address that we had was for Juan's mother. Will said, "I doubt that he will be dumb enough to go there but it is all we have. I figure this guy is on his way out of the state now that he knows we have arrested his buddies."

I knew the neighborhood where Juan's mother lived. It was com-prised mostly of low income illegal immigrants. This was but one of the many neighborhoods in the Norcross area occupied predominantly by renters from other countries. These areas also house numerous gangs, drug dealers, houses of prostitution, and other nice groups of people. If you were to drive down the street in one of these neighborhoods, you would probably feel the urge to lock your doors. The streets are unlit at night. Junk cars are scattered up and down the streets and in people's driveways. If you cracked your window, you would get a whiff of that third world country smell of untended trash lying in the street and yards. You would probably hear some Latin music blaring from some-one's stereo.

After I got the information from Sergeant Will, I had four of my guys change out of their uniforms into plain clothes and check out two of our undercover cars. I had them park on opposite sides of the target house, a couple of houses up. In this neighborhood, everybody parked in the street, so they did not attract any attention. I had a takedown team of myself and three other officers stationed just outside the neighborhood in our marked police vehicles. We were all heavily armed. In addition to our duty pistols (Glock 17's), we also all had AR-15 rifles. This is the civilian version of the military M-16 rifle and fires a .223 bullet. I kept my rifle beside me in my police truck, muzzle down, so I would have quick access to it. My SWAT guys had their issued submachine guns (H & K MP-5's). I also had a ballistic shield if things got really nasty.

Our plan was to try and confirm if Juan was at his mother's house. If we knew for a fact that he was inside, we would just surround the house and order him to come out. If he didn't, we would send the SWAT Team in to get him. The other possibility was that Juan might try and leave and we would take him down on a traffic stop. We would prefer to get him this way. If he stayed in the house, too many other factors came into play. We did not know who all was in the house and we did not want them getting in the way. If we could get Juan outside, it was unlikely that he was going to elude us.

The surveillance team let me know that there were some lights on in the house and it was obvious that someone was home. The only question was whether or not Juan was in there. It was quiet for about an hour or so. One of the guys on the surveillance team called me and said that a car had just pulled up to the target house. A man had gotten out and gone into the residence. They had pictures of Juan but they were too far away to determine if this was him or not, so we just kept waiting and watching to see what would happen next.

After about twenty minutes, my Nextel beeped again. "Hey Sarge, two guys just came out of the house," Officer Chris told me. "One of them is carrying a baby and a duffel bag. I can't be sure, but I think it is our guy." The guy that drove the car there got into the driver's seat. The newcomer got into the backseat with the baby. The car was a white Nissan Sentra. The surveillance team told us that the car was leaving and gave us a direction of travel as they pulled out of the subdivision onto the main road. The takedown team was positioned perfectly.

I had eyes on the Sentra within moments of them pulling out of the neighborhood. The plan was to let the suspect vehicle get at least a mile from the neighborhood before we made the stop. After we had gotten down the road far enough, I activated my blue lights. The other members of the takedown team did the same and spread their vehicles out in a fan behind me. That would provide us with a better cover in case Juan decided to go out in a blaze of glory. I was very conscious that there was a child in the suspect vehicle. I also knew that Juan was wanted for Murder, was considered armed and dangerous, and could not be allowed to get away.

The driver of the Sentra pulled over onto a side residential street. I left about two car lengths between our vehicles. I grabbed my rifle and took cover behind my car door. Officer James yelled at the driver first to step out of the vehicle. There was a bit of a language barrier. The driver was an illegal Hispanic guy who did not speak English. He did understand the tone of what we were saying to him, though, and when he saw all the guns being pointed at him, he got the gist of what we were telling him to do. He exited the Sentra and came back to us with his hands up. He was quickly handcuffed, searched, and secured in a police car.

I then yelled at the other male in the car. I told him to get out with his hands up. We then heard a voice in heavily accented English, "I have my daughter in the car. Please don't shoot. I am getting out."

I yelled back, "You step out and leave her in the car. Do what we say and no one will get hurt." A short, muscular, heavily tattooed subject with a shaved head stepped out with his hands up. He had on a white wife-beater t-shirt and blue jeans. We had him walk back to us. He was handcuffed, searched, and also secured in a police car. His wallet contained his El Salvadoran ID card. It was Juan. The guy who had said either he would kill the police or the police would kill him was taken into custody with hardly a whimper.

Officers checked the car carefully to make sure no one else was hiding there. A female officer had heard us making the stop and came over to see what was going on. I entrusted the baby to her until we could make arrangements for someone to come and get her. The little girl was about two years old. The driver of the Sentra did not have a driver's license and was arrested for that.

I opened the backdoor of the police car where Juan was sitting and told him that he was under arrest for Murder. He did not seem surprised. He did ask me for a favor, though. He said, "Can I please say goodbye to my daughter? I may not see her for a long time."

Juan had not given us any trouble at all and this was a reasonable request. We had made contact by phone with Juan's mother and she was on the way to pick up the little girl. Juan was handcuffed with his hands behind him as he sat in the police car. I had the female officer put the little girl on Juan's lap. When we did this, Juan, the tough, hardened, gang member started crying. He spoke softly to his daughter in Spanish for a few minutes until his mother got there. She took the baby and I told her what I knew about Juan's charges.

After she left, it was time to transport Juan to the jail. Another officer was doing the transport. Juan looked at me and said, "Thanks, man. Thanks for letting me say goodbye. You didn't have to do that."

I noticed that he still had tears in his eyes. *So, even a hardened gang member gets choked up over saying goodbye to his daughter,* I thought. That small act of kindness really impacted him. When the detectives interviewed Juan later that night, he freely confessed to his part in the killing of the rival gang member. He also provided some information about some other unsolved crimes. Of course, he wasn't involved but might know who was. I am sure that he tried to make some kind of deal with the District Attorney's Office. At the end of the day, however, Juan was sent away for a long time.

30

Kidnapped!

OUR NORMAL SHIFT IN Crime Suppression was 5:00 in the afternoon until 2:00 in the morning. That was the peak timeframe for most of the crimes that we dealt with. I had just gotten to the office one afternoon in May of 2009. I noticed several detectives from the Violent Crimes Unit in our assembly room. They had a Hispanic lady and teenage boy with them.

Sergeant Will saw me come in and walked over. He said, "We are probably going to need your guys' help in a little while. We are working a kidnapping case and I think we are about to get a break."

He related the rest of the story to me. The woman that was there had gotten a phone call a few hours before from her nineteen year old son saying that he had been kidnapped. The kidnappers were demanding twenty thousand dollars for his release or they were going to kill him.

This was another new trend that we were seeing more and more of. Our department had been involved in working a number of these types of cases over the last couple of years. Most of them turned out to be drug related. In one case, our SWAT Team was set up in a parking lot where money was going to be traded for the victim, only instead of giving the kidnappers money, they were going to try and arrest them. It had turned into a shootout with our SWAT Team killing one of the kidnappers, arresting the others and rescuing the hostage.

"Is this drug related?" I asked Will.

"Probably," he answered. "The kid who got kidnapped may have some involvement in drugs, but I don't think his mother knows anything about it."

The woman was seated at a table on the other side of the room talking to a detective. The teenager was her other son and was acting as the translator for his mother. She was probably around forty years of age but looked ten years older. Her skin was dark from working outside and her face was weathered. She was shabbily dressed and did not look like she was profiting from the drug trade.

"Do these clowns really think that this woman is going to come up with twenty thousand dollars?" I asked Will.

He answered, "Believe it or not, part of the game is bargaining. We gave her a counter offer to give them. They just called back before you got here and she gave it to them. She offered them five thousand dollars, some jewelry and her car. They said they will call her back in a little while and let her know if that is acceptable."

While we were still talking, the Mexican woman's cell phone rang. The detectives had it wired so they could hear and record the conversation. She talked for a few minutes in Spanish and then disconnected. Her son translated for us, "They say that they will accept five thousand dollars, the car, and the jewelry. They will call back again with where they want the car dropped off."

What kind of jewelry did they think that this lady had? I wondered. She looked like one more, poor illegal immigrant who had come to the United States looking for her pot of gold. From the look of things, she had not found it yet.

I quickly got the Crime Suppression officers together and briefed them on what we were going to be working on. I had them get three of our undercover cars ready to go. We all took our rifles and other equipment we might need and put it in the vehicles. We would be ready to leave at a moment's notice.

By the time we had our cars loaded and ready to go, Sergeant Will told me that we were set. The kidnappers had called back and instructed the woman to park her car at a specific shopping center parking lot in Norcross, just off of the interstate. She was told to put the money and the jewelry in the glove box and to leave the keys in the car. After the kidnappers had gotten her vehicle, her son would be released.

The plan was for the three car loads of Crime Suppression officers to drive down to the shopping center right away and park so that we would have time to blend in. There were eight of us in three vehicles. We stayed in uniform for this operation. We all did have a cover shirt to put over our uniform shirt while we were sitting in our UC cars. The dark tinted windows of the UC vehicles also helped conceal us.

The woman and her son would drive down a little later. A detective would follow her down in his unmarked car and pick them up after she had parked. They made sure to tell the woman not to leave the keys in the car. We did not want to get into a car chase if we could help it.

I was driving one of the UC cars and had two officers in the car with me. As we were pulling out of the precinct parking lot, I saw the woman getting into a red older model, maybe a 1995, Honda CRV that looked like it had seen better days. It had some body damage and visible rust spots on it. *These are some desperate kidnappers*, I thought.

The woman had been told what side of the parking lot to park on. That was where I had two of the UC cars set up. They would park on either side of the CRV leaving about fifty yards between them and the vehicle. They would be the primary take down team. I parked my UC car just across the street from the shopping center in a small business complex. We were about one hundred yards from where she would park but we would be available if the bad guy tried to run on foot. More than likely he would run right towards us.

We could hear the old Honda CRV coming before we saw it. It sounded like the muffler was about to fall off. *Maybe while these kidnappers are in prison they can get some tips on how to pick their victims*, I thought. After the woman parked the CRV, she and the boy got into the detective's car and they left the area. Since the kidnappers had been using her son's cell phone to call her, she called them and told them that the car was there. They said they would call her back after her son had been released.

We then settled into the surveillance mode. There was no telling how long we would have to wait. We all had a good view of the red CRV. It was parked by itself near the end of a row of parking spaces. After about an hour and a half, the officers that were closest to the CRV saw a Hispanic male walking across the shopping center parking lot. No one saw where he had come from. He had probably been dropped off on the other side of the shopping center. He looked behind himself a couple of times as he walked towards the CRV. When he got to the vehicle, he opened the driver's door and hopped in.

We were all moving. The two takedown teams were on the guy in seconds. Because the victim had the keys, the bad guy could only sit there as several big men with rifles and submachine guns converged on him. He was snatched out of the CRV and thrown to the ground where he was handcuffed and searched. We called for a marked unit to meet with us. The detectives were waiting at the West Precinct which was less than a mile away. The bad guy was transported over there to be interviewed.

While this was going on, Sergeant Will received information that the kidnapping victim had been able to escape. He called his mother from a pay phone and asked her to come and get him. We did him one better. Sergeant Will had a marked unit drive down into Dekalb County, the next jurisdiction over, and pick him up. The victim had been kidnapped out of Gwinnett County but taken into Dekalb County where he had been detained. The officer found the victim at a convenience store parking lot waiting. He was also taken to the West Precinct so the detectives could interview him, too.

The suspect that we had arrested understood clearly that his future was bleak unless he cooperated. He spilled his guts to the investigators. He told them everything that he knew about the kidnapping and everyone that was involved. He gave us the name of the "mastermind" behind the operation: Alejandro. He said that there were other people involved but he did not know their names. The suspect did not know that the victim had escaped. He told us where the apartment complex was that the victim was being held in. Most importantly, the suspect told us where Alejandro lived.

When the investigators spoke with the victim, his story confirmed much of what the suspect had said. The victim told the detectives that he thought he was kidnapped because he owed Alejandro some money. He would not admit to any drug involvement. We sent a couple of Crime Suppression officers in a UC car into Dekalb County to find the two locations. After we verified that they were good addresses, our detectives got with the Dekalb County Police Department's detectives and briefed them on the investigation. All of us Crime Suppression officers were deputized and had state wide arrest powers. However, when going into another jurisdiction, it was always better to let that jurisdiction take the lead. Our detectives were taking out warrants on Alejandro for Kidnapping and a number of other charges. Crime Suppression was going to be going into Dekalb County and setting up surveillance on the two addresses. Our goal was to figure out which one Alejandro was going to be at.

I took a team and set up just down the street from Alejandro's house in an older middle class neighborhood. Another team went to the apartment complex where the victim had been held. The team at the apartment complex sat and watched the apartment for over an hour without seeing anyone coming or going. My team saw right away that we were at the right place. Alejandro's house was lit up and there were several vehicles in the driveway. Evidently, he had a party planned for that evening because car after car pulled up to the house. Six or seven cars pulled up to the residence during the hour that we sat there. Alejandro had to know that his victim had escaped and had gone to the police by now. He did not seem overly concerned about it because it was clear that he was planning on entertaining some friends.

Our investigators had coordinated with the Dekalb County Police Department investigators to have their SWAT team serve the warrants on Alejandro. They wanted us to provide perimeter security on the house while they made entry and served the warrants. Normally, we would have met and mapped everything out on a whiteboard. Instead, I was told over the phone that the SWAT team was on the way and we should be ready to move in as soon we saw them. I had all the Crime Suppression officers staged in their UC cars nearby.

It wasn't long before a couple of marked Dekalb County Police cars pulled into the neighborhood followed by their SWAT truck. Our UC cars pulled up and we all piled out as Dekalb's SWAT guys were rushing up to the house. We all had our rifles or submachine guns and formed a perimeter around the outside of the house. We could hear the SWAT team as they moved through the house securing it. There were several shouts of, "Police! Get on the ground!"

After a few minutes one of the SWAT officers approached me and said, "It's secure, Sarge. We found your boy. We also recovered a gun."

About this time, several of our and several of Dekalb's investigators came walking up. We went in the house and found that the party Alejandro was throwing was a pay-for-view boxing match. He had invited a bunch of his buddies to come over and watch the fight with him. I guess he figured he could afford the pay-for-view after his big haul on the kidnapping. The SWAT Team, however, ruined the party.

Alejandro was a big Hispanic fellow with an enormous gut. He had a shaved head and was covered with tattoos. He was wearing the standard gang attire of a white wife-beater t-shirt and blue jeans. He did not claim any gang affiliation but his tattoos indicated that he was in the 18th Street Gang. The kidnapping victim was in one of the investigator's cars. We brought a few of the other men in the house outside to see if he could identify them. He fingered a skinny Hispanic guy that the victim said was the driver when they grabbed him. He was arrested also.

Our kidnapping victim said that Alejandro had a stainless steel revolver when he was kidnapped. Alejandro had kept the gun pressed to his head until they got him to the apartment where they tied him up with duct tape. The SWAT team had seen a stainless steel revolver in the house. It was secured as evidence.

Alejandro and the skinny guy were transported back to Gwinnett so that our investigators could interview them. Sergeant Will asked me if we could go check out the apartment where the victim had been held. "We don't have a search warrant for that location. Could you take your guys over and do a knock and talk?"

A "knock and talk" simply meant that we would go to the location and see if we could get anyone to the door. If we did, we would ask for consent to search to see if we could see anything that might be evidence. I got my Crime Suppression officers together and we headed that way.

When we got to the apartment complex, the team that had been watching it earlier showed us where the apartment was. All the lights were off but it sounded like someone was watching television. We knocked on the door. This was a "soft" approach. Only a couple of the guys had their long guns out and they stayed in the background. I had my pistol out and behind my leg as did the other two officers at the door with me. A young Hispanic woman opened the door. She clearly was not expecting the police and I could see the fear in her eyes. I asked her if we could come in. She said, "No English."

I motioned inside her apartment and she backed up and shrugged her shoulders. That was good enough for us. We did a quick walk through. There was another Hispanic lady in the apartment and a couple of small children. We did not see anything that looked like our victim had been detained there earlier. Whatever evidence that had been there had been disposed of. I did notice an infestation of large roaches throughout the apartment. Since we could not communicate with the women because of the language barrier and since we did not see anything that looked evidence worthy, we decided to call it a night. The roaches convinced us that we did not want to spend anymore time in that apartment.

All in all, it had been a fruitful night. The kidnapping victim had managed to escape and we had reunited him with his mother. Three kidnapping perps were arrested and a gun was recovered. And last, but not least, the poor mother got to keep her Honda CRV.

31

Twelve Kilos

ONE DAY, ONE OF my Corporals approached me and said that he had gotten a call from the Drug Enforcement Agency requesting his assistance. Corporal Mark had spent a number of years working as a detective in our Narcotics Unit. During that time he cultivated relationships with the DEA, ATF, and the FBI. Even though he had been out of that unit for over a year, he still got periodic calls from the DEA requesting our assistance.

Typically, what the Feds needed was to have a vehicle stopped. While the Feds utilize undercover officers and confidential informants to develop their cases, they also use wiretaps and other covert surveillance methods. The Feds would provide specific information about vehicles transporting large quantities of drugs and would need a marked police car to intercept them. Just a few weeks before, a DEA agent had telephoned Corporal Mark and gave him a detailed description of a car that they wanted stopped. The Feds gave Mark the route that the vehicle would be travelling and a description of the driver, a very fat black male. They said, "We need this guy off the street. He is starting to interfere with a bigger case that we are working. He should have at least one kilo of cocaine in the car with him."

Sure enough, Mark made the traffic stop and got in a foot chase with the driver. The perp tried to toss the kilo of coke and a pistol in a trash can while running away. He was so big, though, he never had a chance. Mark got the bad guy and also recovered the drugs and gun.

So, when Mark told me that the Feds needed a vehicle stopped, I was all ears. The DEA agent told Mark that this Ford Expedition was going to be carrying twelve kilos of cocaine. It was going to be driven to one of the houses that the DEA was monitoring. The Expedition would be pulled into the garage. The garage would then be closed and the drugs would be hidden in the vehicle. Two males would be given the task of delivering the cocaine. These drug gangs always pay two subjects to deliver the drugs. The idea is that they will keep an eye on each other. With that much cocaine, it would be tempting not to deliver it, but to take it and sell it to another buyer. The second person also acted as additional security to protect the load.

The DEA agent gave Corporal Mark the location that the Expedition was going to be leaving and told him that they would phone him when the vehicle started rolling. It was very important, however, that the traffic stop look routine. In other words, we needed to make it look like an "accident" that we just happened to stop this vehicle and find the twelve kilos of cocaine. Mark would be looking for some type of a traffic violation. It might be something as simple as not using a turn signal, an improper lane change, or an improper turn. An equipment violation would work as well. He was looking for any excuse to get the vehicle stopped. After he got it stopped, then he would have to figure out a way to "find" the drugs. One possibility was a Consent Search. Mark could just ask them if he could search the car. If they refused, we could bring one of the drug dogs over and see if he alerted on the car.

Since this traffic stop had to look "routine," we only took three officers. I was not going to sacrifice officer safety just to appease the Feds. At the same time, having three officers on a traffic stop was not that unusual. The plan was that the DEA agent would call Mark when the target vehicle got ready to leave. Mark would wait down the road. When he saw the target vehicle, he would start following at a distance looking for a traffic violation. The other officer and I would be in the area, waiting to hear where the final stop would be.

As it turned out, this was probably the easiest twelve kilos of cocaine that were ever found by the police. When the DEA agent called Mark and told him that the Expedition was loaded and rolling, he also provided the license plate number. Mark ran the tag on his computer in his patrol car. The registration status of the Expedition came back "Suspended." That was a great reason to initiate a traffic stop. Mark called us over the Nextel and gave us the news.

Mark waited until the Expedition was about to drive by a convenience store before turning on his blue lights. They pulled into the parking lot and stopped. The other officer and I were pulling in just as Mark was getting out of his patrol car. As he made contact with the driver,

I stood at the rear of the Expedition and watched the passenger. Both subjects appeared to be Hispanic. The passenger did not even look over at Mark but stared straight ahead.

The driver told Mark that he did not have a driver's license. All he had was his Mexican ID card. Mark got him out and handcuffed him. Just like that, he was under arrest for No Driver's License and Suspended Registration. With the driver under arrest and the tag suspended, the vehicle would now have to be impounded. We could look for the drugs as we conducted our inventory. I had the passenger step out. He was a little Hispanic guy and was so nervous, he was shaking. I patted him down for weapons, but he did not have anything except for his own Mexican ID card. So far, he had not done anything wrong so I just had the other officer watch him.

Whenever a vehicle is impounded by the police, they have to conduct an inventory of what is in the car. This prevents people from coming back later and saying that they had valuables stolen out of their car while it was at the impound lot. The inventory also gives the officers the opportunity to look for contraband. While Corporal Mark was talking to the driver and getting information from him, I started the inventory. I opened the back of the Expedition. It was pretty much empty. The interior of the car was very clean. In the back compartment of Expeditions, there are several small compartments along the side of the vehicle. People store motor oil, jumper cables, tools, or cocaine in them. I opened one of these compartments and a kilo sized brick of cocaine fell out. The passenger was quickly handcuffed and secured in a separate patrol car. Mark and I continued to search the Expedition but did not find anymore cocaine. A kilo was good but we were hoping for more.

On any significant drug arrest, we were required to notify our Narcotics Unit. An investigator came to the scene and we told him what we had. Because these investigators spend so much time working undercover, they wear masks when they conduct interviews. The investigator spoke to both of the suspects. They said that they did not know anything about any drugs. He outlined for them what the next twenty years of their lives in prison was going to look like. They were both shaking even more by the time the man with the black hood got through talking to them.

When the tow truck arrived, we had the Expedition taken to Police Headquarters. Drug dealers are very creative in how they hide drugs in vehicles. The DEA agent was adamant that we would get at least twelve kilos out of this Expedition so we conducted a very thorough search. Underneath the vehicle, we found that the drug dealers had constructed a small compartment under the spare tire. The other eleven kilos of cocaine were hidden in that compartment. The street value for a single kilo of cocaine can range between one hundred thousand to two hundred thousand dollars. When you multiply that by twelve, you can see the significance of an arrest like this.

The two guys that we arrested refused to cooperate with the Narcotics investigators. The dealer that they worked for had them convinced that if they cooperated with the police, he would have their families killed. He would then have them killed, even if they were in jail. They accepted their lengthy prison terms without emotion, hoping that with good behavior, they could be out in ten years.

32

Outsmarting a Drug Dealer

CARLOS WAS MAKING A pretty good living selling cocaine. He was from El Salvador and was in the United States illegally so he was not paying any income tax. He also had a small landscaping business to keep up appearances and to supplement his drug earnings. He lived in a nice middle class neighborhood with his wife and children. Every evening, he would grab fifty or sixty dime bags of powder cocaine and drive to the local Mexican pool hall and sell them. Dime bags contain about one gram of cocaine and sell for ten to twenty dollars, depending on how good the coke is. Carlos was probably making upwards of three thousand dollars a week as the designated coke dealer at Tijuana Billiards.

The first time we met Carlos was kind of a random event. It is common knowledge that a lot of drugs are being sold in the Hispanic clubs. Catching them requires creativity on the part of law enforcement. Crime Suppression officers had conducted periodic walkthroughs of many of these establishments and made numerous arrests for Possession of Cocaine and for Possession with Intent to Distribute Cocaine. After being stung several times, most of the Hispanic bars and pool halls had set up lookouts to watch for the police. They were not particularly good lookouts and we seldom had trouble getting into the bars before they spotted us.

We had not visited Tijuana Billiards in a while, so we planned to check it about 10:00 pm. The last time we had been in there had been about three months before and we had arrested one illegal immigrant for Possession with Intent to Distribute Cocaine and two more for Possession of Cocaine. They were evidently his customers. On that occasion, the seller only had a few dime bags left and several hundred dollars in cash.

Tijuana's security guards also acted as the lookouts. They were always by the front door. They screened the customers coming in, checking them for weapons and were also available for the occasional unruly drunk that they would have to throw out. If they saw the police approaching the business, one of them would quickly slip inside and alert the customers that the police were about to come in. The drug dealers always stayed near the men's bathroom so they could quickly flush their drugs down the toilet.

There were five of us that were going to conduct the walkthrough on this particular evening. We were able to pull behind the shopping center that the pool hall was located in without being seen by the security guards. We parked our police cars back there and approached the business on foot. When we came around the side of the shopping center, Tijuana was only about one hundred feet away. A quick peek around the corner let me see that the security guards were distracted by a very attractive Hispanic girl in a very short skirt. While they were attempting to charm her (or negotiate a price), we started jogging towards the entrance and had covered about half the distance by the time they spotted us.

One of the guards jumped off his stool and was about to grab the front door. Officer Jordan yelled at him in Spanish, "Don't even think about it! Sit back down!" The stunned security guard shrugged his shoulders and sat back down. When we got inside, we fanned out. Officer Jordan and Officer Chris headed for the bathrooms. They needed to get in there quick to prevent whoever was selling from flushing their drugs. The rest of us slowly made our way to the back. We were looking for overt threats, or for anybody that tried to run out.

When Jordan and Chris got to the bathrooms, there were just two drunk Hispanic guys that were actually using the bathroom for its intended purpose. Jordan quickly turned his attention to the well dressed guy who was sitting on a bar stool by the back door, next to the bathrooms. When Jordan said, "Hey, how you doing?" he became visibly nervous and I noticed that his eyes kept darting for the back door. The guy was about forty years of age and well dressed.

He looked at Jordan and said, "No English."

Jordan then switched to Spanish and asked the man if he had any drugs. He shook his head and said, "No."

Jordan asked him in Spanish, "Do you mind if I search you?"

He shrugged and said in English, "Its OK."

While Officer Dave stood close by, Jordan, quickly and expertly patted the man down. In his right front pants pocket, he had twenty seven dime bags of cocaine. In his left front pocket, he had several hundred dollars. Before he realized what had happened to him, our new friend Carlos had been handcuffed. At the same time, Officer Chris had cornered another guy who was very nervous about something. A quick check of his name and date of birth on the computer and he was in handcuffs, too. He had outstanding warrants for his arrest.

Jordan took Carlos out the back door. We retrieved our police cars and secured Carlos in Jordan's. It was obvious that Carlos was selling drugs at the bar. Jordan spoke to him and asked if he wanted to work with our Narcotics Unit. Whenever we arrested someone like Carlos, we always gave them the opportunity to become a snitch for the Narcotics Unit. If they assisted in helping us bag some bigger drug dealers, this would often help in reducing the snitch's jail time. Carlos did not even answer Officer Jordan. He just laughed at him. As Carlos would find out, we would have the last laugh at his expense.

Carlos was booked into the jail for Possession with Intent to Distribute Cocaine. Because he was in the country illegally, he was not given a bond. I figured that he would sit in jail until his case came to trial. I was mistaken. Within a week, Carlos was out of jail. Jordan let me know that Carlos had hired a lawyer who had lobbied for and obtained a bond in the amount of ten thousand dollars for his client. Carlos posted the money in cash and was out.

I figured that would be the last that we would see of Carlos. We assumed that he would skip out and head back to El Salvador, but then again, considering the state of things in El Salvador, he might have decided to take his chances with the criminal justice system here. At any rate, within about six weeks, we received information from one of our informants that Carlos was selling cocaine again at Tijuana Billiards.

My entire squad took this very personally and felt that Carlos was thumbing his nose at us. He was making us look bad so we would just have to bust him again. We knew that the security would be tighter the next time around so we would have to come up with another plan. In Crime Suppression, we often did details in plain clothes. The problem was that this was a pool hall that only catered to Hispanics. Any of us Anglos, or even African-Americans that wandered in wearing plain clothes would stand out like the proverbial turd in the punch bowl. They would know that we were police officers.

A recent addition to my squad became my new secret weapon. Officer Rafael was originally from Honduras but had lived in the United States for about fifteen years. Spanish was his first language so he would fit right in at Tijuana Billiards. We teamed him up with a Hispanic narcotics investigator named Antonio. They would go hang out and play some pool and see what they could see. They would also attempt to purchase some cocaine, if possible. Their main goal, however, was to be our eyes inside the establishment. I had borrowed some additional manpower from another squad and we were waiting nearby for the signal to swoop in. There were twelve of us crammed into three undercover vehicles.

Rafael identified Carlos right away inside the pool hall. Rafael had not been with us on the first bust, but he recognized Carlos from pictures that we had shown him. Carlos was hanging out in the bar, but he did not appear to be selling. Rafael picked out the guy who was selling that night. This guy stayed real close to Carlos. When a customer approached, they would walk into the bathroom together to conduct the transaction. This guy was wearing a bright red shirt, which we came to appreciate later.

While they were in the bar, the plan was for Antonio to try and purchase the drugs. He, after all, was the trained narcotics investigator. As it turned out, Antonio was busy trying to pick up women. While we were suffocating in our packed vehicles waiting for the call, Antonio was turning on the charm with the ladies rather than trying to buy some cocaine. Finally, Rafael, God bless him, got tired of waiting on his partner to act. He approached Red Shirt and dropped some hints that he might be interested in purchasing some cocaine. Red Shirt led him into the bathroom and Rafael bought two dime bags for twenty dollars. Red Shirt told him, "If you need anything else, you just let me know. I'll take care of you."

After he made the purchase, Rafael went back to Antonio and they continued to play pool. Antonio was so distracted by the girl that he was talking to that he had not even noticed Rafael slip away for a couple of minutes. Antonio said, "Hey, amigo, I guess I need to go try and buy some snort."

Rafael said, "Don't worry about it. I already took care of it." Rafael is a very smooth operator and did not want to raise any suspicions. They played pool for about twenty minutes more and then Rafael stepped out onto the sidewalk and called me. He gave me a quick run down on what was going on. He gave clothing descriptions for Red Shirt and for Carlos and told us where they were in the bar.

We were staged across the street. I gave everybody a quick briefing on what Rafael had told me. I gave the officers their assignments and we moved in. Since we were in unmarked cars, we just drove right up to the front of the business. We were out of our vehicles and at the doors before the security guards could react. Red Shirt saw us coming and started for the bathroom. Officer Chris grabbed him and pushed him over a pool table. A quick search turned up six dime bags of cocaine in one pocket and some cash in the other. He briefly struggled to get away but we overpowered him and he was handcuffed.

Officer Jordan smiled at Carlos and said, "Hi, remember me?" He then patted him down but did not find anything. Carlos was very nervous, but he was not holding any cocaine that night. While this was going one, one of the other officers saw one of the bar's security guards try and toss a bag of cocaine behind him. The officer had seen him pull it out of his pocket and, thinking no one was watching him, flick it behind him. The security guard was quickly handcuffed as well.

We checked a few more people but did not find any more cocaine. We were disappointed that Carlos was not holding anything, but we were still arresting two people. The security guard was charged with Possession of Cocaine. Red Shirt was charged with Sale of Cocaine and Possession with Intent to Distribute Cocaine.

Rafael and Antonio stayed in the bar and played another game of pool. If they had left when we did, it might have blown their cover. Rafael told me later that after we left, a number of people, including the remaining security guards, walked up to Carlos and shook his hand and patted him on the back. Rafael told us later, that watching Carlos that night, it was clear to him that he was in charge in the bar. Red Shirt was working for him and Carlos was merely supervising. In this way, he kept his hands clean, but probably still took the biggest cut of the money. This knowledge just made us that more determined to put Carlos back in jail where he belonged.

After about a week, it was time to try again. We had found out that Carlos did not have a driver's license. That was going to be the way that we got him. He had to drive to get to the pool hall. I had Rafael dress in plain clothes again and take one of the undercover vehicles and park near Carlos' home. This was another environment in which Rafael was the perfect man for the job. Any of the rest of us would have attracted attention. He was parked a few houses down from Carlos' house, but could clearly see the front door and the cars in the driveway.

After waiting for an hour, at about 8:00 in the evening, Carlos came out of his house. Rafael saw that he was holding a cowboy hat up against his chest. When he got into his Honda Accord, Rafael saw him duck down out of sight for a few minutes. Then Carlos sat up and started driving. Rafael followed at a discreet distance in his undercover vehicle, keeping us posted on their location. We believed that Carlos was going to head for Tijuana Billiards. He drove right to it. Officer Jordan and I made the traffic stop just as he pulled into the parking lot of the pool hall. Getting Carlos in front of where he worked would send a message to any other drug dealers that they could not be too careful. Jordan had Carlos step out of his car and immediately placed him under arrest for No Driver's License. He was going to jail for that. We were just hoping we could find some drugs to go along with it.

We called for a wrecker to come and impound Carlos' car. Jordan started searching the car. Part of impounding a vehicle involves doing a very thorough inventory of any items of value in the car. This gives us an excuse to check it very closely. I watched Carlos as Jordan was looking through the car. It was obvious that he was concerned. He kept sitting up and craning his neck to get a better view from where he was sitting in the back of the police car. After a few minutes, I heard Jordan say, "I found it."

He had found a cigarette box duct taped up under the dash, behind the steering wheel. When Jordan stood up with the cigarette box in his hand, Carlos dropped his head on his chest in resignation. The box contained sixty six dime bags of cocaine. We weighed the drugs. It was about one dime bag shy of the weight required for Trafficking in Cocaine, a much more serious charge. As it was, Carlos was charged with Possession with Intent to Distribute Cocaine for the second time in six weeks. Because he was already out on bond for the previous charge, there would be no bond this time until his trial, no matter how good his lawyer was.

We let Carlos sit in jail for a couple of days and then Jordan and Rafael went and interviewed him. Rafael had been assigned to the

FBI Gang Task Force for a couple of years before coming to Crime Suppression and still occasionally assisted on joint operations. He still had his FBI credentials. When he and Jordan walked into the interview room at the jail, Rafael showed his FBI badge to Carlos. The drug dealer's eyes about popped out of his head. Rafael told him, "You have pissed off the United States government and now you are going to pay."

At that, Carlos started begging them for a chance to work and set up some bigger drug dealers. Carlos said, "I know who set me up." He identified Red Shirt as the one who had orchestrated his arrest. "I always knew that he was a snitch," Carlos said.

Obviously, this was not true but it goes to show the paranoia that Carlos had lived under. Carlos provided us with the two people that he said he got his cocaine from and then just thought that we would let him go. It does not work that way. Crime Suppression officers took the information that Carlos had given us and determined that he was just jerking us around. One of the houses that we checked turned out to be empty and the other drug supplier lived so far away from our jurisdiction that it really wasn't feasible for us to pursue it.

In the end, we just let Carlos sit in jail until his trial. He will probably take whatever plea that the Assistant District Attorney offers him. He will serve a few years in prison and then be deported back to El Salvador. If he makes the mistake of coming back to America after that, we will get him again.

33

Taking Down a Drug House

ONE OF MY GUYS in the Crime Suppression Unit alerted me that he and another officer had identified an active drug house in Buford. They had been working in the area and noticed a lot of traffic in and out of the location. They went back in an undercover car and sat on it for several hours. They saw car after car pulling into the driveway. The driver would get out and walk up to the front door. A transaction would take place and then they would leave. This went on all night long.

While we knew what was taking place, we had to have some concrete proof that the people in this house were selling drugs and not ice cream cones. Because we worked closely with our Narcotics Unit, I asked for their help. One of their investigators went with the Crime Suppression officers and watched the traffic in and out of the house. The Narcotics investigator then set up a controlled buy with one of his informants. The informant bought some crack cocaine. The informant also told us that while he was making the purchase, he had seen one of the males in the house with a pistol tucked into his waistband.

With this controlled buy, we were able to secure a Search Warrant for the residence. The plan was to wait for a few days before we executed the warrant. This would ensure that we did not burn our informant. We also wanted to prepare adequately to take down this illegal narcotics operation. The officers that initiated the investigation were in charge of finding out as much as they could about the location, suspects, weapons, and any other threats.

The fact that one of the suspects had had a gun allowed us to get a "No Knock" Search Warrant. Most Search Warrants involve the officers knocking on the door and announcing themselves. This gives the suspects time to destroy valuable evidence and also to arm themselves and fight if they have a mind to. A "No Knock" warrant is great because you just show up and smash in the door. This type of warrant usually takes the suspects by surprise and does not give them the opportunity to resist or to destroy evidence, such as drugs. The "No Knock" warrants are only given when there is a history of violence or if the officers know that there is an armed suspect there.

Most of the Crime Suppression officers were also on the SWAT Team so they developed the plan for executing the Search Warrant. We did not know how many people would be in the house when we hit it. The informant said that when he made the controlled buy there were two men and a woman there. One of the men had sold him the drugs. The other stood in the background watching the transaction. He was the one with the pistol in his waistband.

A Sergeant in Narcotics said that he would send some of his people to help us. They would help us secure the evidence in the house and process the prisoners. One of the Narcotic investigators drove by the location and shot video so we could get a good look at the house. In the video, I noticed a large pit bull chained to a tree in front of the house. The informant had said that the dog wasn't aggressive but it was one more thing for us to have to consider.

It was decided that when we executed the warrant, we would use the Narcotics Unit's box truck. We could all get into the back of the truck instead of having twenty police cars roaring up to the location. The "stick" of officers that were going to make entry was going to be composed of twelve Crime Suppression Officers. Another four officers were going to be outside the house securing the perimeter in case any one ran out. These four would drive up in their police cars ahead of us to surround the house.

Our Lieutenant and two other Sergeants were going to be in the street watching, listening, and providing oversight. The Lieutenant was in overall command of the operation. I would be the Sergeant in the stick. I would be in charge of those eleven officers once we got ready to smash the door in. I would be positioned towards the rear of the stick so that I could see what was going on and maintain control.

Each officer had an assigned place in the stick. We spent some time in the assembly room diagramming on the white board where everyone was going to be and discussing their responsibilities. The guy at the end of the stick would be responsible for getting the rolling door open on the truck when we arrived. He would then slot back into line. He would become the last man of the stick, covering our rear. One officer was designated as the "ram man." He would be the third man in the stick and would be carrying the heavy metal door ram. When we got up to the house, he would be the one to smash the door open. While several of us would be carrying rifles or submachine guns, one of the SWAT officers, Eric, was designated as a cover man. He was about halfway down the stick. As we approached the house, he would drop out of line and watch the front windows with his scoped, suppressed Colt M-4. I also designated him and the point man as the shooters if the pit bull charged us. We didn't need all twelve of us shooting a dog. Eric would enter the house and assist after we had made successful entry.

The second officer in the stick, Jordan, was responsible for throwing a flash/bang grenade into the house after the door was busted open. A flash/bang is a non-lethal grenade that is very loud and gives off a bright flash when it explodes. Its purpose is to temporarily disorient anyone exposed to it. These are used by SWAT teams and other special operations units during high risk warrants and hostage rescues. Once the door was open, the flash/bang would go in just ahead of us. It should shock and stun anyone in the immediate area and give us that extra split second to get in unopposed.

After working through these logistics, we practiced exiting the box truck a few times. We worked until we were able to do this smoothly and move quickly into position so that we could breach the door of the crack house. We all checked our equipment one last time. We were all wearing body armor. The SWAT guys put on their even heavier armor over their uniforms. Their armor would stop rifle rounds. The rest of us only had pistol rated armor. Hopefully, that would be enough. We were all carrying Glock 9mm pistols as our standard duty weapon. Half of the team were also carrying Colt M-4's, AR-15's or H & K MP-5 submachine guns. I tucked two extra twenty round magazines for my Colt AR-15 rifle into the outside pocket of my BDU pants. The rest of the team would be armed with their pistols. We did not need everyone to have a long gun because someone would be needed to handcuff and secure prisoners once we got inside.

It was finally time to go. The twelve of us that were going to be making entry at the crack house got into the back of the box truck. There was a handrail running the length of the truck for us to hold onto. A Narcotics investigator would be driving. The one who had set up the controlled buy would be in the passenger seat directing the driver to the right house. He would also be handling all radio communications with dispatch. It is always better to have one person designated for this than to have several people all trying to talk on the radio at the same time. The four officers that would be surrounding the house were staged nearby.

When we were about one minute away from the drug house, the investigator gave the signal over the radio for the units to move into place and cover the four corners of the house. I had warned these four officers about the pit bull, knowing that they would be the first ones there. We had timed it perfectly. As the outside team was moving into place, the truck was pulling up and stopping one house down from the target house. The rear door of the box truck was quickly rolled up and the stick of heavily armed officers was out and moving as the truck came to a stop.

We ran in a single file line up the short driveway to the front door. James, the ram man, stepped up and slammed the heavy metal ram into the door. Nothing happened. He hit it again. The door still did not move. We found out later that the drug dealers had barricaded the door by putting a wooden slat across it and using a metal rod to hold it closed. James slammed the ram into the door again. It felt like the entire house was shaking when he hit the door. Most doors only required one or two hits from the ram to get them open. Fortunately, this was a wooden door. If it had been a metal door, by this point, we would have abandoned the front and gone around to the rear to attempt the alternate entry point. The fourth hit from the ram knocked a hole in the wooden door. Jordan yelled, "Bang!" He tossed the flash/bang grenade through the hole. The explosion was very loud outside. I couldn't imagine how loud it was for those inside.

James slammed the ram home a couple of more times and we were in. Smoke and dust hung in the air from the flash/bang. Officers were yelling, "Police! Get on the ground!" The type of stick that we were using was fluid. Because we did not know the layout of the house, we had to be flexible in how we moved. As I entered I saw a black woman and a black man in the kitchen off to my left. Several officers were already putting them on the floor, with their hands out. To my right, two black guys had been caught in the living room making a transaction. One of them had money in his hand; the other had a couple of bags of marijuana. As we entered, they both tried to cram into a tiny bathroom just off the living room. They were ordered out of there at gunpoint and put face down on the carpet.

There was another door off the living room. We were concerned that additional suspects might have ducked into it. Our element of surprise was gone so the point man, Terry, decided to throw a flash bang into that room. He dropped to his knees to present a smaller target and yelled, "Bang!" He opened the door slightly, tossed the grenade in, and pulled the door shut. The concussion was ear splitting and shook the house. Several officers quickly cleared that room, which turned out to be a bedroom.

There was a stairwell going from the living room downstairs. Several of the team had already cleared the bedroom and laundry room that were located down there. From the time we had made entry, the house had been cleared and secured in less than a minute. The four suspects were all handcuffed and searched. Two of the males had drugs on them. One of them was holding the several bags of marijuana that he was in the process of selling. One of the other men had some powder cocaine in a plastic bag. He tried to toss it but to no avail. They were all taken outside and seated on the driveway and guarded by the perimeter team. For those of us inside, we took a moment to catch our breath and savor the adrenaline rush.

Since we were executing a search warrant, the next phase of the operation involved the search itself. The house was thoroughly examined. In the living room and kitchen there were several pieces of crack cocaine laying out in open view on tables. There were also a bunch of Ecstasy pills on a table in the living room. These pieces of crack cocaine and the Ecstasy pills were photographed were they were found and then secured in evidence bags. In the bedroom that we flashbanged, there was a clothes basket with laundry in it. As we dug through it, I found a white tube sock with about fifteen baggies of marijuana. These were also photographed and secured. We ended up finding more crack cocaine but not the large quantity that we were hoping for. We did not retrieve any weapons from this house.

The woman who was in the house was obviously strung out on crack. She had a couple of active warrants on her, including one for Prostitution. Two of the three guys inside the house had outstanding warrants as well. One had a probation violation warrant and the other had an active drug warrant. All four suspects were charged with Possession with Intent to Distribute Cocaine and Marijuana and Possession of Ecstasy. Oh, and the pit bull guard dog? She took off as soon as we started towards the house. She didn't want to have anything to do with the mean looking men with guns. Smart dog.

34

Last Week in Crime Suppression

MY LAST WEEK IN Crime Suppression was memorable. My promotion had been announced. There were ten of us getting promoted to Lieutenant, along with some new Sergeants, Corporals, and a new Major. In my agency, we don't have the rank of Captain. You go straight from Lieutenant to Major. The promotions were announced but they would not go into affect for another week. After that I would transferred out of Crime Suppression to command a shift at a precinct.

I did not want to spend my last week as a Sergeant hunkering down in my office. That was not my style. I wanted to be out in the field with the guys. This was where I had spent the last year and I wanted to enjoy my last week with them.

Early in the week, we did not have anything big that we were working on, so we did some traffic enforcement around Norcross. On these days, we usually all made at least one trip to the jail. Sure enough, it wasn't long before two of my guys were heading to the jail with prisoners. One had an unlicensed driver and the other had located a wanted person on a traffic stop.

My first traffic stop was on a red Toyota Rav4. I stopped it because there was a piece of cardboard where the tag should have been. It had "Tag Applied" written in magic marker on it. I gave the dispatcher my location and a vehicle description. I activated my blue lights and we stopped in the parking lot of a convenience store. As I walked up to the vehicle, I observed that the driver was a black female. There was a little boy of about three years of age sitting in the backseat. He was seat belted in but was supposed to be in a car seat.

I addressed the driver, "Hey, how you doing? I'm Sergeant Spell. I'm just checking your tag. Can I see your driver's license and registration information?" If she had just bought the car, she had thirty days to get a tag. I knew that this was not the case when I saw the driver's hands shaking. The young woman told me that she had just bought the car but had left all of the paperwork at home.

"That's too bad," I said. "Have you got your driver's license with you?"

She opened her purse and fumbled around with it. I knew where this was going.

She looked at me and said, "I must have left my license at home too. You can check it on the computer."

Shantelle gave me her name and date of birth. I also copied down the vehicle identification number from the car. I asked the driver for the keys. This surprised her but she complied. I didn't want to take the chance on her getting scared and driving away.

When I ran Shantelle through the computer, nothing came back. I knew then that she was lying to me. A check of the vehicle identification number showed that the registration of the vehicle was suspended and there was no insurance on it. It was registered to a female named LaToya.

I walked back up to the Rav4 and asked Shantelle if she had given me the correct information. She assured me that she had. I read everything back to her that she had told me. She said, "Oh, I gave you the wrong year for my birth date." She had told me she had been born in 1982. "What I really meant was 1983," she said.

"How do you not know the year that you were born in?" I asked, enjoying the game.

"Well, sometimes I just forget," she said.

"Who is LaToya?" I asked. "The car is registered to her. The registration is suspended and there is no insurance."

This question clearly stumped Shantelle for a moment. "LaToya is my cousin. It's her car," she finally answered.

"I thought you said that you had just bought the vehicle," I queried.

"No, what I meant was that she had just bought it. It's not my car. It's LaToya's," she explained, not very convincingly.

"Who is the little guy in the back?" I asked. "You know that you are supposed to have him in a car seat. He is too little for a seat belt."

"That is my son. I just picked him up from day care and am going home," she told me.

I went back to my car and ran Shantelle's information through the computer with the new date of birth. I knew she was lying but I wanted to see how far the lies would go. This time a valid driver's license popped up. It was clearly not hers, though. The "Shantelle" on the driver's license was five foot two and weighed one hundred and sixty pounds, short and chubby. The girl that I had stopped was tall, about five foot ten and weighed maybe one hundred and forty pounds. She was using Shantelle's information but obviously was not Shantelle.

At this point, I asked the driver to step out of her car. I told her I wanted to show her something on the computer. Before she knew what was happening, I had her handcuffed, searched, and in my backseat. The issue now became what to do with her little boy. For the time being, I let him sit in the backseat with his mother, whoever she was.

I asked the woman who we could call to come pick her son up. By now, she was crying loudly and begging me not to take her to jail. She refused to answer my question about who to call and just kept wailing. I let her scream for a while and started my inventory of the vehicle. I had a wrecker coming to impound it. Under the driver's seat, I found her wallet. She must have forgotten that she had left it under there. In the wallet was an ID card. "Shantelle" was really LaToya. When I ran LaToya through the computer I found out that her driver's license had multiple suspensions. She also had two active warrants. One was for Failure to Appear from her last arrest and the other was for Probation Violation. No wonder she did not want me to know who she was!

By now, LaToya was starting to run out of energy and she had stopped wailing. I told her that I would give her one chance to give me a phone number to call someone to come and pick up her son. If she did not, I would place the child in the custody of a foster home. She would then have to go to court to regain custody. At that, she gave me the name and number of the child's father. When I made the call, I got a voice mail. That was not promising. LaToya then told me that her eighteen year old daughter lived nearby but did not have a car. I called Officer Jordan to come and assist me.

When Jordan got there, he loaded the little guy in his back seat and drove him to his sister's apartment. He wasn't happy to leave his mother and he had her lungs. Jordan said the child screamed the entire trip. At least the problem of what to do with the child was solved.

I knew that my tow truck would be with me soon so I needed to finish my inventory. As I continued to look through LaToya's Rav4, I heard a car door open. I looked up and heard LaToya yell, "I am not going back to jail." With that she was out of my police truck and running. She had managed to get her handcuffs around her legs and in front of her. My window lock had not been on and she had put her window down, reached out and opened the door and was now running as fast as she could.

I can't believe this, I thought. *What a rookie mistake not to have my windows locked!* I had not been in a foot chase in years. Now at forty six years old and a little heavier than I was when I was twenty six years old, I was being forced to exert myself. LaToya had about a twenty five yard head start on me and she was running hard. I told the dispatcher that I was in a foot chase as I tore off after her. She went around behind the convenience store, which was at the end of a small plaza of other businesses.

At first, I was just trying to keep her in sight. I wasn't gaining on her because she was fueled with adrenaline. I knew that would not last, though. As we approached the end of the plaza, there was a grassy embankment that went down about five feet to the parking lot of the next plaza of businesses. We had been running for about one hundred and fifty yards and she was starting to slow. I was only about ten yards behind her now as she went down the embankment. She lost her balance and tumbled head over heels, landing hard on her back.

I rolled her over so that she was face down and handcuffed her again behind her back. I took a moment to catch my breath and then pulled LaToya up and started back to my police truck. She kept trying to pull away so I grabbed one of her fingers in a painful joint lock. It didn't hurt unless she tried to get away but she would end up breaking her own finger if she kept resisting.

By the time I got her back to my truck, several other officers had joined me, including Officer Jordan. He said, "What happened? I leave you alone for five minutes and you are getting into trouble and chasing people."

I laughed and told him about my rookie mistake of not locking my windows. As the wrecker loaded up LaToya's car and I started to the jail, I made sure they were locked. On top of the active warrants for LaToya, and the new charges that I had: Suspended Driver's License, Suspended

Registration, No Insurance, Giving a False Name, and Failure to Restrain a Child, she was also being charged with Escape and Resisting Arrest. In the end, she spent about six months in jail, and I found out that I can still run if I have to.

It was only two days later that I found myself in another interesting situation. On this evening, we were patrolling an area that was getting torn up with residential burglaries and home invasion robberies. It was just getting dark when I saw the white work van driving slowly by a couple of houses. It started to turn into a driveway and then pulled back out onto the road. Maybe the driver had seen me and decided to keep going. I decided to follow and see what they were doing.

The van continued up the road but I noticed it weave once across the center line, and another time onto the shoulder. At that point, I thought that I might have an intoxicated driver. I told the dispatcher I was on a pullover and turned on my blue lights. The van pulled into the parking lot of a Hispanic grocery store and pulled into a parking space.

The driver of the van spoke first as I walked up to his open driver's window, "No English." I guess he thought I would just let him go because he didn't speak English.

"Licencia y registro, por favor," I asked in Spanish.

"No tengo licencia," he answered.

When he told me he did not have a driver's license, I opened the driver's door and motioned for him to step out. "Arrestado por no licencia," I told him. I then instructed him to turn and around and put his hands behind his back. And then, just like that, the fight was on. The short, stocky Hispanic man did not want to go to jail. When I told him to turn around, he said, "No," and started trying to move away. I pushed him up against the van and grabbed for his arm. It was like trying to hold onto a bucking bull. He started jerking and pulling in an attempt to get free. I found out later that he had been playing soccer all afternoon. He was sweaty and slippery and I could feel his arm slipping out or my grasp.

I knew if this guy got free, I would never catch him. He could probably run all the way back to Mexico without getting tired! I had to do something quick or I would lose my prisoner. As he continued to pull away, I stepped towards him quickly and using his own momentum, threw him into the closest object at hand, a newer model Volvo that was parked two spaces over. He slammed into the passenger door hard and collapsed to the pavement. I had heard the breath get knocked out of him.

As I moved in to affect the arrest, my new friend stood up and assumed a boxer's stance. *So, that's how it's going to be*, I thought. *Well, let's go.* Before he could throw a punch, however, I grabbed him in a Thai clinch. This is when both of my forearms encircle his neck and my hands are locked behind his head. I threw two knees into his midsection. Actually, the first one hit him in the groin and the second one hit him in the midsection. The second knee hit him so hard that it lifted him off the ground. I felt the breath go out of him again. I then turned sideways and slammed him down on the pavement so that I could handcuff him. He landed face first in the parking lot. This time, I was able to get him handcuffed and searched without any more problems. He did not have anymore fight in him.

Now that I had him handcuffed, I went ahead and requested back-up. This was the first opportunity that I had had to get on the radio. The situation had developed so quickly there just had not been time. As I was getting the guy up to secure him in my police truck, I could hear someone speaking to me angrily in Spanish. I turned around and saw a middle aged man standing next to the Volvo holding a bag of groceries. When I looked closer, I could see that the passenger door of the car was caved in, in the shape of a man. *That guy really hit that car hard*, I thought. *That was a good move!*

After the prisoner was secured, I walked over to the agitated man. I got the feeling that it was his car that got smashed up. He had a ten year old boy with him that was probably his grandson. The boy translated for his grandfather, "He say that you hurt his car. How he going to fix it?"

I told the boy, "You tell him that it is going to be OK. The county government will take care of it and fix it for him." I got all of their information so that I could forward it to the branch of the government that handles these kinds of claims. I took a few digital photos of the car to go with my report.

When my backup units arrived, one of them was fluent in Spanish. I asked him to get my prisoner's information. The guy did not have any ID on him at all so there was no telling who he was. He gave the other officer his name, date of birth, and address. We both felt that he was probably lying because of how he hesitated when answering the questions. It didn't matter. I was going to put an ID hold on him at the jail.

They would take his fingerprints and send them off to the FBI. He would stay in jail until we determined who he was.

The name he had given us was Pedro. He had several abrasions on his face from getting slammed on the asphalt but no serious injuries. He was pretty indignant about it. He told the Spanish speaking officer that I had beaten him up because he was Mexican and it wasn't right. The officer told Pedro in Spanish that it didn't matter if you were white, black, or Hispanic. If you fought with the police, you were going to get hurt.

As it turned out, Pedro had lied to us and given us a false name. His correct name was Javier. He had three active warrants out for him. They were for Probation Violation, Failure to Appear, and Battery, from where he had beaten his girlfriend up. I also charged him with Driving without a License, Giving a False Name, and Resisting Arrest. Javier's future was not very bright. He was probably going to spend at least six months in jail on his charges and then was going to be deported.

*9 7 8 1 6 0 8 9 9 6 9 6 4 *